*The land movement in Tullaroan, County Kilkenny, 1879–1891*

# Maynooth Studies in Local History

SERIES EDITOR    Raymond Gillespie

This volume is one of six short books published in the Maynooth Studies in Local History in 2004. Like their predecessors they are, in the main, drawn from theses presented for the MA course in local history at NUI Maynooth. Also, like their predecessors, they range widely over the local experience in the Irish past. That local experience is not simply the chronicling of events that happened within a narrow set of administrative or geographically-determined boundaries. Rather it encompasses all aspects of how the local communities of the past functioned from the cradle to the grave and from peer to peasant. The study of the local past is as much a reconstruction of mental worlds as of physical ones, where people agreed and disagreed over the way in which their world was to operate, and learned to live with consensus and division. The subject matter of these six short books includes the social context of marriage and of death in two very different settings and touches on many human activities between those rites of passage. Politics and dancing, both discussed in these books, may seem to be worlds that have little in common but at a local level both activities provided social gatherings at which people met and interacted, exchanged ideas, collaborated or disagreed, and made local societies work. In other cases disputes about how community assets such as common land are to be divided up can lay bare the often unspoken assumptions that local communities have about their world. Understanding such assumptions, which is best done on the spatially restricted level of the local community, remains the key to reconstructing how people in the past, at many levels from townland to nation, lived their lives. Such work is at the forefront of Irish historical scholarship and these short books, together with the earlier titles in the series, represent some of the most innovative and exciting work being done today not just in local studies but in Irish history as a whole. They also provide models which others can follow and adapt in their own studies of the reality of the Irish past. If they communicate something of the excitement of the vibrant world of Irish local history today then they will have done their work well.

*Maynooth Studies in Local History: Number 55*

# The land movement in Tullaroan, County Kilkenny, 1879–1891

Edward Kennedy

FOUR COURTS PRESS

Set in 10pt on 12pt Bembo by
Carrigboy Typesetting Services, County Cork for
FOUR COURTS PRESS LTD
7 Malpas Street, Dublin 8, Ireland
e-mail: info@four-courts-press.ie
http://www.four-courts-press.ie
and in North America for
FOUR COURTS PRESS
c/o ISBS, 920 N.E. 58th Avenue, Suite 300, Portland, OR 97213.

ISBN 1–85182–819–2

Printed in Ireland by
ßetaprint Ltd, Dublin

# Contents

# Acknowledgements

I am sincerely grateful to my research supervisor, Dr Terence Dooley, Department of Modern History, National University of Ireland, Maynooth, for his assistance, guidance and suggestions while I was working on this study. I would also like to thank Dr Raymond Gillespie, series editor Maynooth Studies in Local History, for his advice while editing the original text and for his direction during the MA in Local History course.

I am also grateful to Mr Michael O'Dwyer, Honorary Librarian, Kilkenny Archaeological Society, Rothe House, Kilkenny, for his help and direction while researching in the library at Rothe House and to the staff who voluntarily open the library to the public.

Thanks also to the following: the staff of Kilkenny County Library, especially those in the local history section; the staff at the National Archives of Ireland and the National Library; the staff at the John Paul II Library, National University of Ireland, Maynooth; and the staff of the library at Maynooth Outreach Centre, St Kieran's College, Kilkenny.

I would like to thank my wife, Eileen, and my family, Niamh, John, Lachtain and Éadaoin for their patience while the project was ongoing. I am also grateful to the following people: Mr Edward Young, local historian in Tullaroan for his assistance; Mr Michael Kirk, Tullaroan, for information and a photograph of his grandfather; Mrs Celia Kennedy, Freshford, for providing a photograph of her grandfather. Sincere thanks also to photographer Terry Campion, Freshford, for his expertise and technical help.

# Introduction

The land movement of the 1880s and 1890s is well documented in Irish historiography. T.W. Moody's *Davitt and Irish revolution*, Samuel Clarke's *Social origins of the Irish land war*, William Vaughan's *Landlords and tenants in mid-Victorian Ireland* are examples of well-known works which analyse the events of the period in great detail. Yet, William Feingold wrote in 1983 that one area of inquiry has received much less attention than it deserves, namely, 'the actions and attitudes of those people at the grass roots who made the [Land] League a mass movement'.[1] He made these comments when presenting a statistical analysis of the Tralee poor law union election of 1881. However, because Feingold concentrated on the statistics of the election, even he failed to tell the story of those at the 'grass roots'. Excellent as the analysis is, he names only four local people in his essay and we learn very little of what they actually did during the election campaign.

Earlier studies of the prominent figures who formed the national leadership during the land movement of the 1880s and 1890s, such as Charles Stewart Parnell, Michael Davitt, John Dillon and Timothy Healy, left the impression that the masses below were mere passive players responding to the actions and ideas at the top. One of the aims of this study is to show that this was not always the case, at least not in relation to the people of Tullaroan, Co. Kilkenny.

Tullaroan is a parish in north-west Kilkenny, on the Kilkenny-Tipperary border. It is a rural parish with an area of over 13,600 statute acres. In the decades preceding the land agitation of the 1880s, the population of the parish fell from a total of 3,490 in 1841 to 1,260 in 1881. By that yardstick, it was a community in decline as it faced the forthcoming turbulence. Yet before the end of the decade the community rallied and turned this potential decline around to take a leading role in the land movement in Co. Kilkenny. In the process it became a highly politicized community to the extent that in 1885 the people of Tullaroan would lead the campaign to oust the unionist Lord Ormonde as chairman of the board of guardians of Kilkenny poor law union; in 1888 a number of its inhabitants would face imprisonment under the terms of the Criminal Law and Procedure Act, 1887; by the end of the decade the members of the Irish National League in Tullaroan would feel confident enough to put forward their own candidate for the North Kilkenny by-election of November 1890 ahead of Parnell's nominee and by 1906, as a final indication of their new found maturity, a member of the community would be nominated to represent north Kilkenny in no less a place than the house of commons at Westminster.

The study of rents, price movements and social conditions before and during the land movement of the 1880s suggested that the principal impulse for agitation came from the tenants themselves. Such studies correct the overemphasis on the prominent leaders but they still do not deal sufficiently with the people who joined the local branches to make up the Land League, the Ladies' Land League and the Irish National League. Who were these people? Who were their leaders? What did they contribute to the agitation? How did the agitation affect the community where they lived? What was the effect of the agitation on their families and next-door neighbours? Answers to these questions would enhance our understanding of the land movement. They can only come through concentrated study of the local aspects of the land movement, which is the focus of this short book.

# 1. The establishment of the Land League in Tullaroan

A special meeting of the Kilkenny Tenant Farmers' Association, which had been formed in 1873 to succeed the Kilkenny Farmers' Club, was held in the Assembly Rooms at the Tholsel, Kilkenny on Wednesday 3 November 1880.[1] The purpose of the meeting was to dissolve its constitution, form itself into a branch of the Land League and set about forming branches of the League in the parishes throughout the county. James Cormack, president of the association, chaired the meeting. Among those present were Edward Mulhallen Marum MP and priests from twelve parishes. James Hogan and Philip Kelly represented the parish of Tullaroan. Philip Kelly was actually outgoing treasurer of the Tenant Farmers' Association. He was a tenant with his brothers Edmond and John on 57 acres at Lates, Tullaroan. Edmond also rented 109 acres in Ballybeagh. James Hogan lived in Gaulstown, Tullaroan with his father, Philip, who held 103 acres. Edward Mulhallen Marum MP was the principal speaker at the meeting. In consequence of the depressed state of agriculture Marum advised that it would be an advantage to establish a branch of the Land League. With regard to Co. Kilkenny, he referred to the parishes where there had been difficulties with raising of rents and evictions. Concerning Tullaroan, he felt that all he needed to say was that 'some of the Scullys were known there'. William Scully of Ballycohey, Co. Tipperary, had a notorious reputation as a landlord in Ireland and especially in Tullaroan. In 1865 he attacked a tenant, Bridget Teehan of Gortnagap, Tullaroan, whose husband he wished to evict. He was charged with assault and received a sentence of twelve months hard labour, though there is a doubt as to whether he served the sentence.[2] Marum's remark indicates that there were sufficient reasons in Tullaroan to inspire the founding of a branch of the Land League at that time. The Tenant Farmers' Association was duly dissolved and reformed into a branch of the Land League. At the close of business branches were proposed in 23 parishes in the county. In 20 of them the men requested to undertake the organization of the branches were priests. The Catholic curate of Tullaroan, the Revd Patrick Meany, was named as the organizer there. The first meeting of the new organization, subsequently known as the Co. Kilkenny Central Branch of the Irish National Land League, took place on Wednesday 8 December 1880. The new branches of the Land League already formed in the county were fully represented including Tullaroan, whose representatives were James and

9

Jeremiah Bowe.[3] James Bowe was a tenant on 52 acres at Huntstown, Tullaroan. His brother Jeremiah was not listed as a tenant at this time.

On 11 December 1880 a notice was published in the *Kilkenny Journal* announcing a Land League meeting to be held in Cullahill, Co. Laois, approximately 12 miles from Tullaroan, on Sunday 19 December.[4] The meeting has a place of its own in the annals of the Land League in Co. Laois because it was banned.[5] It attracted a large group of tenants from Tullaroan, led by the Revd Patrick Meany CC, Philip Kelly and at least 25 other men. This is the first list of Land League supporters in the parish. They included John and Edmond Kelly whose holdings have already been accounted for; Columb Kennedy, one of the biggest tenant farmers at that time, who held 189 acres in Adamstown, valued at £155 and 109 acres in Ballyroe valued at £82; William Holohan, a tenant on 110 acres at Rathealy, valued at £97; Patrick Brennan, who held 64 acres at Ballytarsna until 1882 when the lease was taken over by Edmund Brennan. Some of the others held land as listed in table 1.

**Table 1. Holdings of Tullaroan Land League supporters, c.December 1880**

| Tenant | Townland | Holding acres | Valuation £ s. d. |
|---|---|---|---|
| John Gorman | Raheen | 53 | 35 05 00 |
| Sylvester Gaffney | Remeen | 32 | 24 00 00 |
| Patrick Walsh | Brittas | 38 | 26 10 00 |
| Nicholas Nugent | Foyletaylor | 47 | 17 10 00 |
| John Maher | Foyletaylor | 36 | 22 00 00 |
| Michael Maher | Raheen | 24 | 12 00 00 |
| Lacton Hoyne | Liss | 32 | 22 00 00 |
| John Kerwick | Oldtown | 36 | 30 00 00 |
| James Walsh | Rathealy | 34 | 26 00 00 |

*Source:* Cancelled books; Irish Valuation Office; county: Kilkenny; barony: Crannagh; parish: Tullaroan.

This was a representative group of tenants with holdings varying in size from 24 acres to 189. The following also attended the meeting in Co. Laois but are not listed as occupiers of land at this time: Michael Robertson (probably Robinson), Tullaroan; Laurence Coogan, Tullaroan; James Hogan, Gaulstown; Michael Phelan, Brittas; William Hogan, Gaulstown; Edward Grace, Remeen; Richard Morris, Tullaroan; Patrick Walsh, Tullaroan; James Hoyne, Liss; James Grace, Brittas; Kyran Delany, who occupied a house in Courtstown, valued at 10s.

Six weeks later, at the end of January 1881 the Tullaroan branch of the Land League joined in the celebrations following the release, after an unsuccessful trial, of Charles Stewart Parnell and 13 other land leaguers who had been charged with conspiracy to prevent the payment of rent and conspiracy to create hostility between landlords and tenants.[6] The failure of the jury to return a verdict inspired the countrywide celebrations among the supporters of the Land League. Due to bad weather in Tullaroan on Tuesday 29 January the celebrations there were put on hold but: 'They made up for the delay on Saturday night as all turned out and, preceded by the band, paraded the village. Loud cheers were given for Parnell, the Land League, the Tullaroan branch and the Messrs Kelly.'[7]

# 2. Boycotting, imprisonment and division in Tullaroan

O n Sunday 5 December 1880 two notices were posted in Tullaroan village calling on the people to boycott a local tenant, William Dillon, because he had paid his rent on time to his landlord, William Woodroofe.[1] The following week William Dillon accosted two of his neighbours, James Bowe of Huntstown and Michael Meagher of Rathmacan, and accused them of writing and posting the notices. According to the police report, both men allegedly admitted to Dillon that they had done so. Three weeks later, on Christmas Eve, James Arundel Nixon JP, Clone House, Freshford, must have received quite a shock when he opened his post as it included a threatening letter.[2] The letter was unsigned but purported to come from his tenants. It brought the poverty of the tenants to the notice of the landlord. The writer called for a reduction in rent and threatened that if the landlord did not comply his family would have a most unhappy new year and that 'the black night' would come on him when he least expected it; if he did not look to his tenants now, he would get 'the death Lord Mountmorris [sic] got', a reference to the murder of Viscount Mountmorres, which took place near Clonbur, Co. Galway on 25 September 1880. It was said to be a particularly gruesome example of rural ferocity.[3] RIC Sub-Inspector William Lawless of Johnstown Barracks, whose area included Freshford, reported the threatening letter to his superiors on 1 January 1881.[4] According to the sub-inspector, Nixon did not know what to do with the letter so he did not report it to the police. One of the constables in Freshford had heard a rumour of its being received and went to investigate. The letter was handed over to him. As Nixon was not taking any proceedings against any of his tenants he had no idea who had written it. Sub-Inspector Lawless did not believe that Nixon's life was in immediate danger. He felt that a person 'evidently not ignorant' sent the letter but there was no clue as to the identity of the writer.

On Sunday 24 April James Bowe was reported once more to the police by William Walsh because that morning he had allegedly issued another warning to Walsh and to another neighbour, Edmond Walshe of Huntstown, that they were not to give milk to the police.[5] William Walsh reported the threat that evening and added that another neighbour, Pierse Delany [sic], told him that he crossed through the fields to his own house sooner than pass the [police] barracks 'lest James Bowe should hear he had been speaking to the police'. James Bowe was beginning to make a name for himself with the police, but it appears that there were many more people out agitating during that third week of April 1881 in Tullaroan and its environs.

On the previous Friday morning, 22 April 1881, the bell on the church of the Assumption, Tullaroan rang out to summon the people to join a protest against process-serving in nearby Kildrinagh in the neighbouring parish of ✔ Urlingford.[6] At about 1.00 p.m. a crowd of 200 men, women and children proceeded to landlord Michael Keatinge's residence in Woodsgift, approximately four miles from Tullaroan. They were led by fifes and drums and they carried a straw effigy, which was burnt on the lawn opposite Keatinge's hall door. It appears that crowds of people, expecting the serving of writs on Keatinge's tenants, had assembled several times that week. Because of this, Sub-Inspector Lawless was forced to apply for an additional number of policemen to protect the process-server the following day, Saturday 23 April. Lawless accompanied a force of 64 men under the command of Sub-Inspector John Mark O'Brien, of the James' St barracks in Kilkenny, to the townland of Kildrinagh.[7] A crowd of between 200 and 300 men, women and children met the police near the house of Eliza Hoyne, the first to be served with a writ. A number of men prevented the process server from reaching the door. The riot act was read and the police were ordered to turn back the crowd. When the police charged, the crowd cleared. In spite of some severe injuries to a policeman and the process server, no assailant was identified in the subsequent police reports. Though the crowd followed the process servers for the rest of the day, there was no further violence.

When Sub-Inspector Lawless' report of the proceedings arrived in Kilkenny on Monday 25 April, his superiors questioned the fact that no rioters were identified. This forced him to re-evaluate the situation and two days later he submitted a return listing 38 people who could be 'identified by the constabulary for having taken part in the riot' in Kildrinagh.[8] Included were 14 men from Tullaroan who were all recommended for prosecution. The RIC officer made a number of observations in his report about the occupations, character and circumstances of these men and about their behaviour that day in Kildrinagh. Philip Kelly was described as a farmer in good circumstances and of good character and as a member of the Land League. Philip Doheny, Pierce Doheny and Jeremiah Bowe were farmers' sons. The first two were supposedly not members of the Land League. It was not known whether the latter was a member but he was described as a 'drunkard' as was William Holohan. Patrick Byrne was a servant boy of good character but in poor circumstances. Edmond Walshe of Huntstown was allegedly a member of the Land League but James Walshe was supposedly not. Only Philip Kelly was said to have been with the 'mob' on the road that attempted to prevent the police from passing. The 'mob', or someone in it, was alleged to have shouted: 'We'll give them what they got at Carrickshock. We'll have another Carrickshock.'[9] The rest of the men were identified as having been on the road outside the house from where the police were stoned, but none of them were identified as being in the haggard 'whence the stones had come'.

Eventually proceedings were taken against only 21of the 38 named. Three of them were from Tullaroan. The case came before Freshford petty sessions on 20 May. Freshford is six miles from Tullaroan. A force of 100 policemen was on duty that day to help keep the peace. The crown solicitor withdrew charges against five of the accused. The other 16 pleaded guilty and were bound over to keep the peace. They included two women. Bridget Dillon and Margaret Purcell who were convicted of assaulting the process-server. Dillon was fined £1 or one month's imprisonment. The fine was paid. Purcell was sentenced to one month's imprisonment.

The proceedings in Freshford passed off without disturbance, but the affray, which took place in Kildrinagh on 23 April 1881, had serious repercussions in Tullaroan for the rest of the year.

By the end of April 1881, the police in Tullaroan were following the reported activities of James Bowe with keen interest. While his brother Jeremiah was listed among those who attended the riot in Kildrinagh, as was their servant, Patrick Byrne, James was not on the list. Either he did not attend or he escaped notice but the following day, Sunday 24 April, he reacted to the events in Kildrinagh, as already noted, by allegedly cautioning his neighbours, William Walsh and Edmond Walshe, not to give milk to the police. A week later, on Sunday 1 May, Constable James McElhoney of Tullaroan Police Barracks found a threatening notice posted on the wall at Tullaroan crossroads at 10.00 a.m.[10] Half an hour later Sub-Constable Morrissey found three more notices posted on the walls at the chapel gate (fig. 1).

*1* Copy of original boycott notice posted at the gate of
Tullaroan RC Church on 1 May 1881
*Source:* NAI, CSORP, 1881/44511.

The wording was the same on the four notices:

Notice
A thing that ought to be known
Dunnigan's cars carried the bailfs [*sic*] to Kildrinagh

One of the notices had the additional words:

Do not take down this.

The message referred to the recent serving of writs in Kildrinagh. The writer took it upon himself to let the public know that the bailiffs had been carried to the scene by cars belonging to a man named 'Dunnigan'. In his report of the incident to the sub-inspector at Johnstown, Constable McElhoney wrote that he believed the threatening notes were written and posted by James Bowe, who had been involved in the affray in Kildrinagh on 23 April. This was a definite statement of fact concerning Bowe's involvement in the Kildrinagh incident. If it is correct, why was he not named on Sub-Inspector Lawless' list of those who were recognized as having taken part in the riot? Whatever the reason, James Bowe was now in deeper trouble.

The constable was undoubtedly helped in detecting the origin of the notices by the fact that they were written on labels on the backs of which were found the addresses of members of the Bowe family of Tullaroan, Urlingford, and Tramore, Co. Waterford. While not constituting outright proof, these certainly drew the attention of the police to the family and to James Bowe in particular. But the question must be asked – could James have been so naïve as to practically give himself away by making such a mistake? As he demonstrated his adequate organizational capabilities later on – he subsequently became president of the Irish National League in Tullaroan – it is difficult to believe that he made the mistake of writing four boycotting notices on labels, which contained addresses that drew the attention of the police directly to his door. He might miss one address but he could hardly miss four. This raises the question of a conspiracy being initiated, either by the police or others, against James Bowe.

Constable McElhoney also complained that Bowe, his brother and a servant named Byrne were endeavouring to have the police boycotted.[11] (It is noteworthy that the word 'boycott' was being used at this early juncture in a police report from Tullaroan, only eight months after Captain Boycott had suffered the tactics on his Mayo farm.) In light of the fact that the suspicions against Jeremiah Bowe and Patrick Byrne were not mentioned again, it is possible that James Bowe was singled out and targeted by the police as a suspect in order to quell the boycotting that was now becoming obvious. Constable McElhoney was alarmed enough to note in this report that he never witnessed anything as remarkable as the change in the manner of the people towards the police since 23 April, the day of the affray in Kildrinagh. He explained that neither the Bowes nor Byrne, nor any person whom they could influence would speak to the police.

Four days later the occupants of Tullaroan police barracks had more to endure than simply suffering the silence of the people. On 6 May 120 policemen, including the men from Tullaroan Barracks, were drafted into neighbouring Kilmanagh to provide protection to process servers there. The events in Kildrinagh on 23 April meant the police were better prepared for disturbances this time. Once again a crowd between 500 and 600 people gathered and a number of serious incidents took place in the village of Kilmanagh and the townland of Killeen.[12] The police were booed and jeered and stones thrown at them. As a result of this behaviour 18 men, including James Bowe, were charged with a variety of offences ranging from riot to assaulting a police officer. When the charges were brought against the men in July no addresses were given in the newspaper report but it appears that James Bowe was the only protestor from Tullaroan to be charged in connection with those events. Once again the notion of a witch-hunt against James Bowe arises because it was the constable from Tullaroan, James McElhoney, who identified the Tullaroan man and stated that he was in front of the mob that day in Kilmanagh. According to the policeman, Bowe had a heavy pole in his hand and boasted afterwards that he had a good metal spike to fit into it.[13] In a crowd of 500 people he was hardly the only person from Tullaroan yet he was the only person from there identified.

That night, 6 May 1881, a hostile demonstration, including the stoning of the police barracks, took place in Tullaroan. Sub-Inspector Lawless of Johnstown reported to his superiors on 9 May that Constable McElhoney had informed him that he believed James Bowe encouraged the mob that night too.[14] This report went through the county inspector to Dublin Castle. The county inspector suggested that Sub-Inspector Lawless and the resident magistrate for the area should confer about the advisability of arresting Bowe. This conference took place but the resident magistrate, William Hort, wished to consult with Constable McElhoney before making a decision.

Before this meeting was arranged another threatening notice appeared on 8 May.[15] John Brett of Brittas found a notice posted on his door warning him against working for Denis W. Kavanagh who had taken possession of a garden in Tullaroan. Brett worked as a herd for Kavanagh and he and another man were sent to plant the garden with cabbages. He received the following warning, which included a sketch of a coffin so there was no mistaking the message:

See here Mr Britt [sic] if you dig another sod in that haggert [sic] you may dig your own grave and here is your coffin. A land leaguer.

On 9 May Constable McElhoney wrote a damning report of the alleged activities engaged in by James Bowe. He stated that for the previous 14 days Bowe had succeeded in 'creating a state of terror in the minds of the people regarding their intercourse with the police'.[16] The die was now cast for the summer of 1881 in Tullaroan. A week later, on 15 May, yet another notice was posted at the chapel gate. This time it was a direct call to the public to boycott the police.[17] The men of Tullaroan were warned not to stand any more at 'Michael Toban's Cornir'. Michael Tobin was identified in Sub-Inspector Lawless's report of the incident as a dealer whom 'the malcontents in Tullaroan' counted as friendly to the police. Now the public were warned not to stand at his premises any longer and not to supply the 'peelers' with fresh or sour milk or butter. What brought about this change of attitude in the people of Tullaroan to the constabulary? In a report dated 17 May Sub-Inspector Lawless noted that the Tullaroan police had been on duty in Kildrinagh on 23 April and in Kilmanagh on 6 May. The support given by them to the process servers on those two occasions caused their alienation from the people and brought about the change in attitude there. T.W. Moody states that this was a familiar tactic of the League: the mobilising of local people to prevent or impede, short of actual conflict with the police, and bring a maximum of hostile publicity to bear upon the service of ejectment processes and the execution of ejectment decrees for non-payment of rent.[18]

The meeting between Resident Magistrate William Hort and Constable James McElhoney to discuss the question of arresting James Bowe took place on 19 May in Kilmanagh when the resident magistrate attended a petty sessions to issue licenses. In spite of what McElhoney wrote in his report of 7 May, Hort decided not to arrest the suspect for the present because the evidence so far submitted would not lead to a conviction. He suggested that if the portion of the evidence concerning the posting of the notices to boycott the police could be pointed at Bowe, then 'reasonable ground' of suspicion (against Bowe) could be applied for.[19] In fact it transpired that the magistrate met James Bowe that day for the first time. In the course of the licensing sessions Hort announced that he would not grant a license to carry arms to any person against whom charges were pending of illegal conduct at Kilmanagh on 6 May. Since charges were pending against Bowe he was refused a licence and had to surrender his gun. He complained bitterly of having to do so as he was 'suffering the ravages of crows'. Bowe also used this opportunity, while speaking to the magistrate, to accuse Constable McElhoney of being prejudiced against him and in fact he denied that he had taken part in any boycotting proceedings.[20] As things turned out James Bowe did not have to answer charges concerning the 6 May riot in Kilmanagh because, as we shall see, he was otherwise engaged on the day of the trial, which took place in July. Constable McElhoney wrote a confidential character report on James Bowe again on 28 May. This time he outlined the full list of allegations against Bowe dating back to 5 December 1880.[21] In addition to the allegations outlined above, the constable added that Bowe had even warned the Kellys of Lates against conversing with the police.

It will be recalled that the Kellys had received cheers from the people at the Land League celebrations in Tullaroan village at the beginning of February. They were highly thought of. Yet, according to the constable's report, even they were not spared the wrath of James Bowe. Constable McElhoney noted that Bowe sent word to Edmund Kelly by his brother Philip (treasurer of the Kilkenny central branch of the Land League!) that he (Bowe) had seen Mr Kelly speaking to the constable after returning from the Kilmanagh meeting and supposed that he was giving information. Of all the charges made against Bowe perhaps this is the most significant. He obviously felt that if Philip Kelly was to hold a prestigious position on the committee of the central branch of the Land League in Kilkenny, then this meant his family should not be conversing with the police. It was clear that James Bowe, and maybe he alone, had a full grasp of the significance of Land League membership and tactics at this time and that as far as he was concerned there could be no half measures. Constable McElhoney was moved to write: 'This man's arrest would have a very good effect on this neighbourhood.'[22]

The police recommendation was acted upon. On 9 June 1881 a warrant to arrest James Bowe was issued by Dublin Castle under the Protection of Persons and Property (Ireland) Act, 1881. When it became law on 2 March 1881, this act temporarily introduced detention without trial for crimes involving violence or intimidation in a proscribed district. A person arrested under the act would not face trial or be discharged without the direction of the lord lieutenant.[23]

At 3.30 a.m. on 13 June James Bowe was arrested by Sub-Inspector Lawless who wrote in his report that: 'There was no excitement, resistance, nor opposition shown to the arrest.'[24] On the basis that the police hardly announced their intentions, it was unlikely that there would be a reaction at that early hour of the morning. The inspector escorted Bowe to Kilkenny train station, from where he was brought to Newbridge. A telegram was sent to the inspector later that day to say that the prisoner had been safely lodged by 11.30 a.m. in her majesty's prison at Naas, Co. Kildare 'there to be detained during the continuance of the said Act, unless sooner discharged or tried by our direction'.[25]

At the time of his arrest James Bowe was 34 years of age. He was married with two children. His commitment to the Land League could not be questioned. From the beginning of December 1880 his actions mirrored the tactics adopted by the Land League countrywide. He attended meetings and, according to the police, simultaneously carried out intimidation against friend and foe in the persons of his neighbours and the police. Bowe, his brother and their servant Patrick Byrne were said to be 'conspicuous and notorious amongst the people of Tullaroan as extreme advocates of Land League agitation.'[26] The constable believed that Bowe was doing his utmost to prevent the police getting provisions. This issue obviously had a serious effect on police households but they were not the only people to be affected.

When a policeman and his family spent some years in an area, it is understandable that the relationship between them and the community would be reasonably cordial, especially if the locals were in the habit of supplying provisions such as milk and butter. In the great scheme of political oppression such contact would hardly merit consideration, particularly if it meant economic benefit to the community. But times were changing in Tullaroan as elsewhere. James Bowe felt that the local community should have no contact with the police. He was not concerned about anyone's feelings even though some people were in fact saddened by this turn of events as witnessed by the following extract from a letter written by Mrs Walshe of Huntstown to Mrs McElhoney, wife of the constable:

> Scarcely ever in my life have I felt anything so painful as to be now obliged to say to you that I cannot sell the milk to you any longer … But now the spirit of the times has so changed that we can no longer withstand public opinion … Ned feels this if possible more than I do … I assure you dear Mrs McElhoney that the Sargt [*sic*] and yourself are second to none in our personal regard and esteem. Perhaps if the great respect and esteem we have always had for you had not been so well known, such a small matter as the milk might have escaped the long tongues of the neighbours.[27]

In this letter there is confirmation of the good relationship that existed between the police and the community up to this time and the change that was brought about in that relationship due to 'the spirit of the times'. Mrs Walshe stated that if anything this change had more of an effect on her husband, Ned (Edmond). It is interesting to consider the predicament he was in. Later on he would hold the position of joint secretary of the local branch of the Irish National League and later the United Irish League. So, even though it is not possible to be sure, he may have been secretary of the Land League branch at this time and he supplying milk to the protectors of process servers! Perhaps as with the Kellys of Lates, who had been spoken to by Bowe about conversing with the police, Ned Walshe only now realized the significance of Land League membership and that his relationship with the Tullaroan police would have to change. Mrs Walshe's remark about 'tongues of the neighbours' was probably a reference to Bowe whose farm was in the same townland, Huntstown, as the Walshe's. In a second letter to Constable Morrissey, Mrs Walshe wrote that she was sorry to refuse milk to 'people we received so much kindness from always.'[28] There was obviously an emotional impact as well as an economic and social one to be felt by those who had been on good terms with the police. It is clear from these letters that Land League tactics in general, and James Bowe's actions in particular, were the cause of change in relationships, not just between the police and their suppliers but also between neighbours.

Constable McElhoney seemed eager to have James Bowe removed from the scene and predicted that his arrest would have a good effect in the neighbourhood.[29] Ironically in the days immediately preceding the arrest of Bowe things were relatively quiet in Tullaroan. According to Constable McElhoney, this was due to the fact that Bowe's wife was ill for some days towards the end of the month which implied that Bowe alone was responsible for the pursuit of these tactics. The constable's report left the resident magistrate under the impression that the intimidation had finally stopped. That this implication was incorrect was corroborated by the magistrate himself in an assessment of the situation some few days after Bowe's arrest: 'The consequence of his arrest has been the renewal of the ill-feeling towards the police and their being again boycotted.'[30] So with James Bowe behind bars, there was confirmation that others were involved in the intimidation. By July the ill feeling manifested towards the constabulary at Tullaroan barracks continued in its worst form.[31] By now the police were, in their own words 'completely boycotted'. The resident magistrate was moved to write: 'I know of no part of it [my district] where so much exasperation shows itself as at Tullaroan.'[32]

For his first three weeks in gaol James Bowe's health and conduct were good.[33] On 6 July, he submitted a request for release. His application generated a large amount of correspondence over the next few months. One issue concerned the discharge itself. Sub-Inspector Lawless made it clear that both he and Resident Magistrate Hort believed the release of James Bowe now would much endanger the peace of the neighbourhood.[34] The second issue that arose from James Bowe's request for release concerned his handwriting. Sub-Inspector Lawless wanted to find out if James Bowe had signed and dated the request for release himself. He needed this information because the resident magistrate and he had concluded that this handwriting appeared to be identical with the handwriting of anonymous notices posted in Tullaroan on 1 and 8 May.[35] He specifically stated in his report that if it was shown that the document was signed by Bowe then the resident magistrate felt that it and the threatening notices should be shown to an expert to find out if they had been written by the same person.

A question arises as to who drove this issue of the handwriting. A letter from Resident Magistrate Hort accompanying the inspector's report made no mention of the handwriting issue. It is possible that it was discussed orally by the two men and Sub-Inspector Lawless then felt free to use the magistrate's comments in his report but, because of its seriousness, one imagines that Hort would have made some reference to it in his letter. In the absence of any such mention it appears that it was Lawless who pushed the issue of the handwriting. Once again the question of prejudice raises its head. The police in Tullaroan and in the district office in Johnstown seemed determined one way or another to keep James Bowe in prison.

On 17 July another threatening notice was posted at the chapel gate in Tullaroan in which the labourers of landlord William Scully of Gortnagap were warned 'not to work for him or hold intercourse with any in his employment'.[36] With James Bowe still in gaol, who was responsible for posting this notice? For the second time in two months the name of Michael Meagher of Rathmacan is mentioned in a police report.[37] Once again there was no proof but the sub-inspector believed that he wrote and posted the note. He was a tenant of William Scully on 44 acres in Rathmacan.[38] Later on, like James Bowe, Meagher too would make his mark in the Irish National League and especially in the United Irish League. Irrespective of the police suspicions no action was taken against Michael Meagher. In spite of the threatening notice, three unnamed labourers hired themselves to help save the hay, which indicates that not everyone felt obliged to follow the dictates of the local Land League. There is no record of any repercussions for those who defected.

Over the next few weeks the authorities looked at the consequences that might arise from releasing Bowe against the backdrop of the continuing hostile situation in Tullaroan. At the same time they investigated the question of Bowe's handwriting. The resident magistrate considered the question of release. Only 10 days had elapsed since his last report but he felt: 'Tullyroan [*sic*] district was never in a worse condition as regards boycotting and opposition to the police than it is now.'[39] He practically admitted that Bowe's arrest was a mistake because the situation had intensified since then. A further shock for the authorities arrived from an unexpected quarter. The Tullaroan district dispensary doctor, Michael A. Warren, informed the sub-inspector that he would be declining to attend the constabulary barracks any longer. The resident magistrate remarked that it was believed the doctor was 'acting under terror'.[40] The feeling of disappointment at this turn of events is palpable on reading the magistrate's report. There is no record of the doctor reporting intimidation. If he had done so it would surely be mentioned as evidence. Either he felt intimidated enough to withdraw his services from the barracks or else he too had joined the ranks of the protesters. The boycotting campaign undoubtedly received a shot in the arm when this news broke. There was another development mentioned in this report that would have given the Land Leaguers a further boost had they been aware of it. Resident Magistrate Hort had reached the stage where he was now looking at reasons that could be advanced for Bowe's release! Included in these reasons were: that he made the appeal and denied the charges; that he was an industrious man and that his enforced absence from his farm was an injury; that the mutinous spirit of the neighbourhood could not have arisen solely from his action as it was now manifested in a worse form than when he was at large.

This conciliatory tone may have prompted Sub-Inspector Lawless to highlight the handwriting issue in his report. He was convinced that Bowe wrote not just the two notices of 1 and 8 May but, in fact, all of the boy-cotting notices posted in Tullaroan up to 15 May.[41] By the end of July the inspector realized that James Nixon, who, it will be recalled, had received a threatening letter at his home in Clone House, Freshford the previous Christmas Eve, was also an agent for a property in Tullaroan.[42] Now the police inspector believed that James Bowe wrote the Nixon letter too. With the handwriting investigation still under way and in spite of the resident magistrate's conciliatory suggestions, James Bowe's application for release went unanswered and he remained a prisoner into the month of August.

By mid-August there was no improvement in the feeling of the people towards the police.[43] Even though James Bowe had applied for release as far back as 6 July, the authorities found no grounds to accede to the request. The handwriting expert John Peake made his report in mid-August. He was unable to form an opinion such as would be safe to act on.[44] Even this did not hasten Bowe's release. Then there was an unexpected turn of events, which brought some hope to the constabulary.

A meeting of the local branch of the Land League was held in Tullaroan on 16 August. Fr Patrick Meany CC, vice-president of the League, dropped a bombshell at the meeting when he denounced the conduct that James Bowe had been guilty of 'as calculated to bring disgrace on the League'.[45] The priest went so far as to say that Bowe was better off in prison! Needless to say the constable was able to report that this attack, 'coming from a quarter so unexpected, caused great disappointment to the troublesome section around this village.' He predicted that the development would have a good effect.

Resident Magistrate Willam Hort was astounded by this 'about turn' by the priest. He was of the opinion that Fr Meany was 'one of the greatest firebrands in the county'.[46] No evidence has come to light in either the local newspapers or the Chief Secretary's Office Registered Papers to support this assertion. As already noted, the priest attended the Cullahill Land League meeting on 19 December 1880 as part of the Tullaroan group of supporters. He addressed another meeting in Cullahill on 10 July 1881.[47] There was no disorder on any scale at this meeting so it is difficult to understand why he was labelled a 'firebrand'.

As a result of the priest's criticism James Bowe's family posted notices at the chapel gate saying they would not accept any pecuniary or other aid from the Tullaroan branch of the Land League in future.[48] This excited the constable who predicted that: 'Now there is a split in the ranks I expect we have passed the most troublesome times.' He was correct in his observation regarding the existence of a split between the Bowes and the Land League, but his prediction regarding the future was incorrect. The absence of violence in the community continued into September and this might have indicated to the authorities that they were indeed past the 'most troublesome times'. But by the end of the month it was clear that opinions had changed little.

On the evening of 30 September James Grace visited the constabulary barracks in Tullaroan. He spoke to one of the men and said he was willing to give milk and butter when he could get a car. He then left the barracks and entered a public house in the village. The next day he made a statement that someone in the public house had burnt 'a squib of gunpowder' in his face.[49] The police report gives the impression that Grace made a full statement but the sub-inspector later stated that Grace refused to name any person who was in the public house or to say anything about it. The police only heard about the incident from another source so it appears that Grace had learned his lesson well. In fact Sub-Inspector Lawless believed that the powder was actually fired from a gun and not 'burnt' in his face. He also stated that Grace was intimidated because he was seen talking to the police and because he offered provisions to the police. This was precisely what happened back in the month of May when Constable McElhoney accused James Bowe of creating a 'state of terror' in the minds of the people. So the reality was that by October the situation in Tullaroan had not changed at all. The message to the people was still the same – have nothing to do with the police – and James Bowe was far removed from the scene of the crime. Yet, to the probable chagrin of the Bowe family, there were no further arrests at this time either.

By now Resident Magistrate Hort was in a dilemma. Early in October he considered the case for releasing James Bowe once again but he had learned from Constable Doyle of Tullaroan that 'they [the people] seem to be repenting of having partially relented.' He was getting milk but 'with a bad grace.' This created turmoil for the resident magistrate. He would unhesitatingly recommend the discharge but for the ill feeling to the constabulary. His attitude to James Bowe had definitely softened because he questions if 'it is desirable to detain so petty a prisoner when so many have been released'.[50]

In mid-October RIC County Inspector James Gibbons enquired about the boycotting situation in Tullaroan. He asked to be supplied with the names of the culprits.[51] Constable Thomas Doyle informed the county inspector that the shopkeepers in Tullaroan would supply the police with groceries, bread, butter and anything they had for sale but 'no person in the place will supply the police with milk'.[52] He added that the people were quiet in their behaviour around the police station but that the ill feeling still existed. This is the first intimation we get that the shopkeepers in general were supplying provisions and it raises a question regarding Constable McElhoney's description of events. He seemed always to paint the worst picture while Constable Doyle at least had some good news for the higher authorities. Resident Magistrate Hort obviously took this as a step forward and wrote that though the situation was not all that could be wished for it showed a marked improvement in the feelings there. At last he could write: 'I am personally of opinion that James Bowe might now be discharged.'[53] The recommendation from the resident magistrate was taken up though it would take another week before the discharge notice was signed. This was dispatched from the Chief Secretary's Office in Dublin Castle to the prison in Naas on 27 October with instructions that the prisoner be issued with a 'heavy warning' and that his movements be watched by the constabulary who should report at once any grounds for suspecting him to be engaged in any illegal proceedings.[54] The warning hardly concerned the prisoner as the governor paid his car and railway fare and sent him home.[55]

No doubt James Bowe received a heartfelt welcome from his family after four months' imprisonment. A large crowd assembled at his residence that night and the police were informed that Bowe addressed them. In fact during his first week of freedom the police carried out their instructions to the letter and kept a keen eye on him. Ten days after returning home Bowe was the subject of a distinctly biased police report but this time, luckily for him, a more circumspect acting-county inspector, Alex Read, dealt with the correspondence generated. This man proved to be a more demanding official who did not accept 'hearsay' and 'conjecture' as evidence.

On Sunday 6 November a notice was posted at the church gate in Tullaroan while the people were attending last Mass. Head Constable John Depo wrote a confidential report on the incident and stated that James Bowe, recently released from Naas Prison, was believed to have posted the notice.[56] The constable wrote: 'In fact the posting of it *is solely attributed to him because there were no such notices, nor any having an illegal tendency posted in or about Tullaroan during the period of Bowe's detention.'* There was also an allegation in this report about a speech Bowe made when he addressed the crowd that had assembled at his residence on the night of his liberation. He allegedly told his audience that he would be guilty again of the same offences for which he was previously arrested. On Monday 7 November an immense number of people, according to Depo, helped Bowe to thresh and save his crops and the rumour that a neighbouring band was to have attended that night to wind up the proceedings also made it into the constable's report.

This report was incorrect in one important respect. As previously mentioned a threatening notice was posted in Tullaroan in July while Bowe was in prison. To emphasize the import of Depo's accusation the offending piece was underlined in the original letter. This may have been done by Constable Depo himself or, more likely, by County Inspector Read when he read it the following day. The new county inspector was not impressed by the details and he dealt with it in a different manner from the way previous reports were handled. For the first time the contents of a report were questioned. The inspector commented that the suspicion regarding the posting of the notice

was 'very indirect'.[57] He noted that the statement concerning Bowe's alleged
speech to the people on the night of his return seemed to have been made on
hearsay only. Finally, Inspector Read asked if any of the police were present at
that gathering and, tellingly, if not why not? Before signing off, the inspector
even asked for additional information on the non-appearance of the band.

There is another reason for believing now that Bowe did not post the
notice on 6 November. The offending notice is in the form of a 'No Rent
Manifesto'. It was written on the lines of the better-known 'No Rent
Manifesto' issued on 18 October 1881 from the central branch in Dublin,
which was signed by Charles Stewart Parnell and six other Land League
leaders, namely A.J. Kettle, Michael Davitt, Thomas Brennan, John Dillon,
Thomas Sexton, and Patrick Egan. This was the manifesto, which gave William
Forster, the chief secretary, 'an excellent excuse' to proclaim the Land League as
an unlawful and criminal organisation on 20 October 1881.[58] Only Patrick
Egan, the national treasurer of the Land League, signed the notice posted in
Tullaroan. As an official document, presumably sent to all branches, it must
have been for the attention of the local officials and was probably posted in
Tullaroan by one of them. It has already been mentioned that a split existed
between the Bowe family and the local leaders. In this case it is hardly
possible that, in the week immediately following his release, James Bowe was
given access to branch documents thereby enabling him to 'post the notice'.
He could not return to Tullaroan on 28 October and within a week be in a
position to orchestrate this action.

Head Constable Depo's answers to the questions raised by County
Inspector Read raised the issue of the split between James Bowe and the
vice-president of the Land League branch, Fr Meany. The band did not turn
up at James Bowe's house on the night of the threshing because the priest
requested them not to. No doubt this development added to the strain
between the Bowe family and the Land League leader; however, the band
may not have been missed because the people who had assembled during
the day in question were obviously intent on enjoying the occasion anyway.
They spent the evening cheering and shouting around the village and
remained 'till a late hour'.[59] By so doing, the people not alone showed their
support for Bowe but also their disdain for the actions of the priest.

An intriguing fact regarding the noisy group that gathered in Tullaroan
on the night of Bowe's release came to light in December when James Bowe
wrote a letter to the local paper to thank his neighbours for helping to bring
in his crops when he was released from prison. In the letter he stated that the
majority of those who helped were from the neighbouring parish of
Kilmanagh. Bowe questioned the attitude of his fellow parishioners and did
not mince his words when commenting on the leaders of the local branch.
To understand the depth of James Bowe's feelings, the letter is reproduced in
full:

Dear Sir – You will kindly allow me to return my sincere thanks to the many kind friends who assembled to dig and secure my potato crop immediately on my release. As it might naturally be expected that those in my own neighbourhood should be the first to give me whatever assistance I might require, I think it right to state that the help I received was rendered principally by friends from a distance. I feel, therefore, it due to them to record their patriotic action. I am not able to explain why this work was left undone by the people of my native place. It may be that they had no sympathy for a 'suspect' or at least that the 'leaders' in the locality have none. To the 'good men and true' of Coorstown, Killeen and Kilmanagh, I desire to express my thanks. – Yours very truly, J. Bowe.[60]

James Bowe's confidence in publishing this letter was remarkable. He was unafraid to state his case and unconcerned about the feelings he might generate. He lays the charge that there was no sympathy for him firmly against the 'leaders' in his own locality. Here he must have been referring to the curate, Fr Meany. As he had shown before his imprisonment when he warned his neighbours against giving supplies to the police, Bowe let no one off the hook, no matter what his or her position in the community.

It is understandable that James Bowe would now turn his attention to his family and his farm. He spent every day of the third week in November working the farm and visited John Walsh's public house three times during the week.[61] This was his old haunt where he was supposed to have plotted much mischief before his arrest but, according to the police, his visits now were not by arrangement with anyone else. The police kept a close watch on him as instructed. Head Constable Depo did not indulge in conjecture when reporting these matters to his superior. He simply noted the above observations and, in his only comments, stated that Bowe still exhibited the same defiant bearing towards the police which he showed before his arrest and that 'he does not seem to have as much influence with the people since his release as he formerly possessed'.[62] There was no accusation against Bowe and the allegation regarding the posting of a notice on 6 November was not mentioned again. Because of the split between James Bowe and the leaders of the Land League, the police finally accepted that he was no longer engaged in any boycotting or other illegal association. In this way ironically he bene-fited from the split, which may have compensated somewhat for the fact that he had suffered most during the land war in Tullaroan.

The land war has been described as the campaign of agrarian protest, com-mencing in 1879, in which tenant demands for rent abatements in consider-ation of a serious downturn in agricultural incomes were transformed into a campaign against landlordism *per se*.[63] British Prime Minister William Ewart Gladstone's incoming government of 1880 acknowledged the need for

2 James Bowe, Land League activist, held as a 'suspect' in
Naas gaol, 13 June–28 October 1881.
*Source:* Mr Michael Kirk, Huntstown, Tullaroan, grandson of James Bowe.

concession and this resulted in the Land Law (Ireland) Act 1881 becoming law on 22 August 1881. This act gave legal status to the longstanding tenant demands known as the 'three Fs'. These were: fair rents, free sale, and fixity of tenure. One of the most important elements of the act was the establishment of the Land Commission, which came into being on 20 October 1881, the same day the Land League became a proscribed organisation. The Land Commission adjudicated on fair rents and made loans of up to 75 per cent of the purchase price of land available to tenants wishing to become owners. The lower rents caused the deflation of the land war in the autumn of 1881.

As the year came to a close, Tullaroan was quiet and peaceable. There was an improvement in the bearing of the people towards the police who were able to get milk, butter and fuel openly.[64] Land agitation quietened for a time before activities resumed again with the formation of a branch of the Irish National League. This would turn out to be a more politically orientated movement than its forerunner in the parish. However, the following year it was the ladies of Tullaroan who took the limelight.

# 3. The Ladies' Land League and the 'ruthless hand of the evictor'

Early in 1881 Michael Davitt wished to ensure that the funds of the National Land League would continue to be disbursed to evicted tenants if the existing leaders of the League should be imprisoned. Thus on 26 January 1881 he persuaded the Land League executive to sanction the formation of a provisional central committee of ladies headed by Anna Parnell, on the precedent of the Ladies' Land League founded in New York by Fanny Parnell the previous October.[1]

The first newspaper report of a meeting of the Tullaroan branch of the Ladies' Land League appeared in the *Kilkenny Journal* of 15 April 1882. The meeting took place on the previous Sunday and was chaired by the vice-president, Mrs Bowe, wife of James Bowe. It is noteworthy to see Mrs Bowe in this role a few months after she had turned down help from the Land League branch in the parish because of the criticism levelled at her husband by the vice-president, Fr Meany. Either the split between the Bowes and the league was healed or the ladies were determined not to allow it to affect their deliberations. Carter states in relation to Queen's County that 'The petty jealousies and rivalries which plagued the men's branch seemed not to beset the women.'[2] This was the case in Tullaroan too because the secretary of the ladies' branch was Mrs Walshe, wife of Edmond Walshe. She was the lady who wrote to Constable McElhoney in Tullaroan police barracks the previous May stating her regret at being forced to cease giving milk to his family and decrying 'the tongues of the neighbours'.[3] Ten months later she was now willing to work as a fellow branch officer with those very same neighbours and perhaps more significantly they were willing to work with her.

The main business of the meeting on 15 April was to set up a fund for the testimonial to the Revd Thomas Feehan. He was the only priest from Queen's Co. to be imprisoned during the land war of 1879–82.[4] At the next meeting, chaired this time by the president, Mrs Meagher, the sum of £28 was handed in for the Revd Feehan Testimonial. £8 17s. 6d. was gathered in members' subscriptions, £5 of which was sent to Miss Parnell and £3 17s. 6d. to the Prisoners' Sustentation fund. These were quite substantial funds and this aspect shows how active the branch was, interested not just in local matters but prepared to be involved in affairs beyond the parish. A resolution was passed condemning the government for failing to take steps 'to stop the cruel hand of the evictor'.[5]

## Table 2. Members of Tullaroan Ladies' Land League, July 1882

| | | | |
|---|---|---|---|
| Miss Phelan★ | Brittas | Miss Grace | Huntstown |
| Mrs Grace★ | Remeen | Miss Maher | Huntstown |
| Miss Walsh★ | Rathealy | Miss M. Grace | Ballyroe |
| Mrs J Maher★ | Foyletaylor | Mrs Teehan | Lisnalea |
| Mrs J Kerwick★ | Oldtown | Miss M Purtill | |
| Miss Kerwick★ | Oldtown | Miss B Young | |
| Misses Hoyne★ (2) | Lissballyfroot | Mrs Tobin | |
| Mrs Walshe★★ | Huntstown | Mrs Dillon | |
| Miss M Walshe★★ | Huntstown | Miss Maher | |
| Mrs Bowe★★ | Huntstown | Miss Bowden | |
| Mrs Meagher★★ | Curragh | Mrs Holohan★ | |
| Mrs Hogan★ | | Mrs Young | |
| Miss Hogan★ | | Miss E. Grace | |
| Misses Purtill | | Miss K. Maher | |

Those marked ★ were from the same families of the men who attended the Land League meeting in Co. Laois on 19 December 1880 (Table 1).

Those marked ★★ were the wives of members of the first Irish National League committee formed in March 1884 (Table 3).

Source: *Kilkenny Journal*, 22 July 1882.

The Ladies' Land League was exclusively made up of wives and daughters of ✓ tenant farmers.[6] This raises a question of elitism concerning the branch, which did not include any members of labourers' families.

At the height of the summer the Tullaroan ladies were forced to turn their attention to home as 'the ruthless hand of the evictor' fell on one of their own. On Thursday 13 July 1882 Ellen Forde, neé Stapleton, a widow living alone, was evicted by Denis W. Kavanagh JP, who resided at Balief Castle, in the neighbouring parish of Urlingford. This was the second occasion in ten months that Kavanagh raised the hackles of the people of Tullaroan. He caused the posting of a threatening notice in July 1881 when he took possession of a garden in the townland of Brittas. Now the 'cruel and heartless action of the landlord in razing this miserable cabin' was condemned at a meeting of the Ladies' Land League in Tullaroan on Sunday 16 July when arrangements were also made to rehouse the evicted tenant.[7] Anna Parnell wrote that apart altogether from the tenants' right to houses, [rebuilding] houses acted 'as a permanent sign and symbol that all power did not lie with the foreign enemy in possession of the country.'[8]

The parishioners of Tullaroan started to build a new house for the evicted tenant almost immediately. A traveller, passing the scene on the day the rebuilding commenced, was so impressed by the sight that he put pen to paper and complimented all involved in a letter to the newspaper. This writer described the poor widow who was evicted as 'very weakly in bodily health and said by all to be mentally affected'.[9] A very poor picture is painted of the entire eviction episode involving all aspects from the destruction of the old hovel, to the mental state of the widow and the questionable intentions of the landlord. The situation was milked for its full propaganda value.

On Sunday 30 July 1882 Ellen Forde was installed in her new 'castle'. The occasion was 'a splendid and in some ways affecting' demonstration which took place under the 'blaze of a July sun.'[10] A dramatic three-line heading appeared over the report in the *Kilkenny Journal*:

The Widow Forde's Castle.
A Touching Demonstration at Tullaroan.
Noble Work of the Lady Land Leaguers.

Among those present at the handing over of the new home was Revd Patrick Meany CC (mistakenly recorded as Neary) and Mr James Bowe, 'ex-suspect'. This indicates that the tension that existed between Bowe and the Land League leader was at an end, or at least had softened, by this time. Two policemen also basked in the sun by the roadside. In noting that James Bowe was an 'ex-suspect' the reporter gave him an elevated status. Donal J. O'Sullivan writes that persons arrested under the terms of the Protection of Person and Property (Ireland) Act 1881were regarded as heroes in the community and obtained overnight notoriety. Some of them in later years inserted 'ex-suspect' after their name as their title and claim to fame.[11]

In the report about the rehousing of the evicted tenant, the lady Land Leaguers of the parish received glowing praise for coming to the her assistance. They had defied 'the law's tyrant' and ignored the possibility of having to suffer 'the hardships of a felon's cell' in their exertions to 'assist their distressed and wronged fellow countrymen and women.' Stimulated by the 'noble example' of the ladies, the men of the parish joined in the work.[12] The result of this coming together was that within a few weeks a 'fine, comfortable and commodious house' was produced for the widow.

The 'poor widow' returned thanks and 'hoped that she would never again experience a visit from the crowbar brigade who had frightened her almost to death but that she would be allowed to live in peace'. If the good lady was capable of delivering that oration she was hardly 'weakly in bodily health' or 'mentally affected' as described by 'A Correspondent' in his letter two weeks previously. It is clear that those supporting the injured party in the eviction scene were once again making full use of the propaganda machine in the battle for public opinion. To be fair to the proprietors of the *Kilkenny Journal* they gave Denis Kavanagh, the offending landlord, ample space in the issue of 29 July to state the facts of the case as he saw them. He was also given an opportunity in the corresponding issue of the rival unionist newspaper, the

*Kilkenny Moderator*, to state his case where the editor wrote that the landlord was entitled to publish his position in every organ open to him. The report about the rehousing of the evicted lady on 2 August was not the end of the matter. Also in that edition of the paper was a long letter from the Revd Patrick Meany CC in which he answered charges made by Denis Kavanagh in the 29 July issue. This letter reveals a little about the character of the man described the previous October by Resident Magistrate William Hort as 'one of the greatest firebrands in the county'.[13] His astuteness is evident as he picks off Kavanagh's arguments regarding the 'falsehoods' put about by the priest and others concerning the eviction. Kavanagh had threatened legal consequences for the priest because of these charges but Fr Meany made the allegations concerning the eviction again in this letter. There is no evidence that he suffered in the courts at Kavanagh's hands for repeating the falsehoods so we must assume that the priest had the upper hand in the debate. We can also deduce from this letter that the priest, notwithstanding that he had been labelled a 'firebrand', was in fact supportive of the payment of rent. He refers to two of Kavanagh's other tenants who had 'paid their rents punctually' but were about to suffer the same fate as the Widow Forde. His derision was reserved for the landlord who, in spite of the fact that the rent was paid, had already served legal notice to the two tenants and was preparing for further evictions. This also helps us to understand the stance he took against James Bowe's extreme actions the previous summer. It is clear that Fr Meany was not a radical and therefore he would have had difficulty in accepting the boycotting measures taken the previous year in Tullaroan.

Following their success in rehousing the Widow Forde, there are no more reports about the activities of the Tullaroan Ladies' Land League. However, unlike their counterparts in Queen's Co. whose role in the land struggle, according to Carter, ceased after 1882, the Tullaroan ladies reformed in 1888.[14] In August the most influential branch in Co. Kilkenny, Castlecomer, had been dissolved.[15] It can be presumed that the Tullaroan branch went the same way. In her introduction to *The tale of a great sham*, Dana Hearne notes what Anna Parnell wrote of the relationship between the Ladies' Land League and the national leadership of the Land League itself: 'From the start there was a marked and constant hostility displayed by the Land League executive towards the Ladies' Land League.'[16] This culminated in the dissolution of the Ladies' Land League in August 1882. It seems a tame demise for what was, at local and national level, a vibrant organisation. By mid-1882 a change had come about in Tullaroan. The punctual payment of rent in May that year was not met with the intimidation that greeted similar action in December 1880. The tension that existed between former protagonists had softened, if it hadn't disappeared altogether. The accommodation between Charles Stewart Parnell and Prime Minister Gladstone, known as the 'Kilmainham Treaty', and the arrears act of 1882, which became law in April, brought an end to most of the agitation around the country. From the tenants' point of view the arrears act complemented the land act of 1881 and between them enough was conceded to them to take the steam out of the anti-landlord movement.

However, a year later, at the end of 1883, the editor of the *Kilkenny Journal* warned his readers that it would be false to infer that under the operation of the land act the farmers of Co. Kilkenny 'have settled down contentedly.'[17] The editor congratulated the citizens of the county that the criminal business 'for the present assizes is trifling' but the observation that the remarks made by several of the judges 'that recent land and other legislation has been so beneficent as to establish calm' was followed by the warning that it was 'a delusive calm'. A resurgence of agitation in 1884 coincided with the growth of the Irish National League, which had been founded in October 1882. When the land agitators of Tullaroan eventually responded to the challenge of the new organisation, they did so with even more enthusiasm than they displayed previously. The venue for the next clash was in the nearest elected assembly, namely, the meeting rooms of the Kilkenny poor law union.

# 4. The impact of the Irish National League on Tullaroan

The Tullaroan branch of the Irish National League was founded at a meeting held in the grounds of the Roman Catholic church on 2 March 1884.[1] The Revd Walter Walsh CC explained the rules for the formation of branches and impressed upon the audience the necessity of uniting with and assisting their fellow-countrymen in their legitimate struggles for land law reform and self-government. All the reports concerning the setting up of the Irish National League emphasize that it was established in October 1882 primarily to advance the cause of national self-government and only secondarily to promote land law reform.[2] Yet, in Fr Walsh's mind, and in the minds of his listeners, land law reform was seen as the more immediate issue of the two at this time. Referring to 1885 and 1886 Laurence Geary states: 'To them [the Irish farmers], the prospect of legislative independence was secondary to the more pressing problem of rent and falling prices.'[3]

The following were unanimously elected to the respective offices at that inaugural meeting: the Revd Thomas Hennessy PP, president; the Revd Walter Walsh CC, vice-president; Edmond Kelly, treasurer; Edmond Walshe, secretary; Henry J. Meagher, assistant secretary. At the next meeting, a week later, a committee was elected by ballot. James Bowe was returned first with the highest number of votes, which suggests that the rift between him and the members of the former Land League was definitely at an end. Over 50 members were enrolled at this meeting.[4] Two additional members, Columb Kennedy and Michael Teehan, were unanimously elected to the committee at the next meeting in order to have the different districts of the parish 'satisfactorily represented'.[5] The holdings of the committee members indicate that the Irish National League in Tullaroan represented large and small farmers (Table 3).

A county convention of the Irish National League was held on Thursday 17 April 1884. The Revd Walter Walsh CC, Edmond Kelly, Edmond Walshe and Henry J. Meagher represented Tullaroan. The following resolution was passed at the meeting:

> that we urge the Nationalist Party in Ireland to avail themselves of public positions open to them and request that they will send their representatives to the Poor Law Boards, Corporations, Town Commissions and all other boards and thus destroy the landlord ascendancy too often practised at the meetings of our public bodies.[6]

**Table 3. Holdings of Irish National League
committee members, March 1884**

| Tenant | Townland | Holding | Valuation £ |
| --- | --- | --- | --- |
| Edmond Walshe | Huntstown | 126 | 109 00 00 |
| Henry J Meagher | Briskalagh | 46 | 29 00 00 |
| | Curraghscarteen | 115 | 100 00 00 |
| Edmond Doheny | Ooldtown | 116 | 83 00 00 |
| James Clohosey | Tullaroan | 36 | 30 10 00 |
| William Dillon | Ballaybeagh | 276 | 90 00 00 |
| John Tone | Rathealy | 31 | 9 00 00 |
| Michael Teehan | Gortnagap | 126 | 36 10 00 |
| Columb Kennedy | Adamstown | 189 | 155 00 00 |
| | Ballyroe | 109 | 82 00 00 |
| James Bowe | Huntstown | 52 | 35 10 00 |

*Source:* Cancelled books, Irish Valuation Office; county: Kilkenny; barony: Crannagh; parish: Tullaroan.

This call had been made first by Charles Stewart Parnell as far back as 1881 and the resolution was more a reflection on Co. Kilkenny than on the national situation as the Kilkenny poor law union, which included the city and some of the surrounding parishes, was particularly lax in answering the call. Arthur Butler, marquis of Ormonde, was returned year after year as chairman of the board of guardians. Tullaroan was in the Kilkenny poor law union area and this resolution seemed to catch the imagination of the newly formed Irish National League branch whose members immediately saw an opportunity to avail of the political system to strike at the power of the gentry. The branch got involved in its first political campaign when the position of coroner in north Kilkenny became vacant due to the death of James Fitzgerald on 30 April 1884.[7] Meetings of the Irish National League in Johnstown and Tullaroan dealt with the vacancy. Resolutions were passed at meetings of both branches referring to the call made at the county convention that every public appointment should be filled only by those whose principles were in accordance with the 'National programme'.[8] The concerted approach by the branches to filling the coronership was not required on this occasion as all of the candidates were 'of the same creed and of the one political principle and there was no immediate necessity for any interference'.[9] Dr Mullally of Gowran, a supporter of the Irish National League, won the election.

Next the Tullaroan branch turned its attention to the board of guardians. When it was introduced in 1838, the poor law was a limited measure intended to provide a safety net for the destitute.[10] The country was divided into 130 unions, with a workhouse in each, and 2,049 electoral divisions (later increased to 163 unions and 3,438 divisions). Boards of guardians were composed of elected guardians, chosen by those paying poor rates and local magistrates sitting *ex-officio*. The poor rate was levied on both owners and occupiers of land in equal measure and both groups were granted votes. The proportion of *ex-officio* guardians was increased from one-third to one-half following the 1843 Act exempting occupiers of property rated at less than £4 per annum from the poor rate. Elections took place annually.

On 15 June a specially convened meeting of the Tullaroan branch of the Irish National League took place.[11] The members adopted a resolution calling the attention of the branches in the county to the composition of boards of guardians and especially to the 'glaring and unaccountable fact that the responsible position of chairman was held by landlords or their nominees'. The branch members pledged themselves to return as poor law guardians none but members of the Irish National League who would pledge themselves to support exclusively members of the league for the position of chairman, vice-chairman and deputy vice-chairman of the boards. The branch also condemned the unpatriotic action of several of their neighbouring branches in north Kilkenny who had ignored this resolution, which had come from the county convention.[12]

At the end of November 1884, Edward Mulhallen Marum MP announced his decision to resign from parliament. The issue was discussed at the Tullaroan branch meeting held on 30 November. It was hoped that Mr Marum would be prevailed upon to reconsider his decision and a strong opinion was voiced that a convention should be held immediately 'to consider this most important question in all its phases'.[13] This suggestion drew favourable comment in the *Kilkenny Journal* where it was noted that: 'The practical suggestion of the Tullaroan branch of the Irish National League that a convention should be immediately summoned for the purposes of considering Mr Marum's resignation has met with ... approval and support.'[14] Once again their confidence in providing a lead to the county on an important issue is noteworthy. At a convention held in January 1885 Marum was prevailed upon to reconsider his decision to resign.[15]

The meeting of the Kilkenny poor law union to elect the chairman of the board of guardians for 1885 took place on Thursday 2 April.[16] The sitting chairman was the marquis of Ormonde. He was the first to be nominated for the position, proposed by Sir John Blunden, Castle Blunden, Kilkenny, seconded by Alderman John Francis Smithwick JP, Kilcreene Lodge, Kilkenny. Smithwick was sitting MP for Kilkenny city. The nominee for the elected guardians was an *ex-officio*, John P Hyland of Clonmoran, Kilkenny. He was proposed by Martin Morrissey PLG, a member of Kilkenny city branch of the Irish National League and seconded by Edmond Kelly PLG of Tullaroan. To the consternation of the proposer and seconder, Hyland declined to stand.

There was great disappointment at this turn of events. The editor of the *Kilkenny Journal* stated: 'It was a miserable piece of bungling from start to finish.' Only 16 of the 28 elected guardians attended. Meanwhile the neighbouring union, Urlingford, had joined Callan, Thomastown and Castlecomer, the other unions in Co. Kilkenny, in returning nationalist chairmen.

At the next meeting of the Irish National League in Tullaroan, the branches whose guardians had stayed away were called upon to demand an explanation from the 'twelve cowards'.[17] The Tullaroan members recognized that the real problem lay with the guardians themselves not all of whom could be depended upon for their support. The members of the Tullaroan branch were determined that it would not fail for the want of organization next time round.

On Sunday 21 March 1886 the new Irish National League committee in Tullaroan called on the elected guardians of the Kilkenny union 'to meet on the next Fair day to make all necessary preparations with regard to the election of chairman for said union for the coming year'. Once again the *Kilkenny Journal* was impressed with 'the excellent suggestion made by the Tullaroan branch of the National League'.[18] The year before the branch had simply called on the elected guardians to return a nationalist chairman. This time the members would organize a meeting beforehand to make arrangements. In the next issue the importance of securing the position of chairman was emphasized:

> It is a chairman's duty before putting any question to the meeting to consider whether such question is one fit to be put and if he is of opinion that it is not, to decline to put the question. This decision places immense power in the hands of all chairmen of boards of guardians and is an additional reason why the National League should use strenuous efforts to elect a gentleman representing them in politics as chairman of the Kilkenny union … the suggestion put forward by the Tullaroan branch should be acted upon.[19]

The meeting took place on 29 March. Journalists were refused entry. The editor of the *Kilkenny Journal* accepted that this was necessary so as not to inform the supporters of Lord Ormonde of the strategy to be adopted by the nationalist guardians. To his amazement, however, a report of the meeting was published in the following edition of the rival *Kilkenny Moderator* which caused the *Journal* editor to agonize on the identity of the person who was 'guilty of such a breach of faith as to supply all the particulars to the Orange newspaper.'[20] The *Moderator* had reported that as a result of the meeting Edmond Kelly PLG of Tullaroan would be proposed for the chairmanship of the board of guardians.[21] Only eight elected guardians attended the meeting. The *Moderator* correspondent hoped that it wasn't necessary to remind each member of the board who felt that the marquis should be re-elected to attend punctually at the board meeting the following day.

The headline in the Kilkenny Journal editorial the day before the election took place read:

'FLUNKEYISM OR NATIONALITY – WHICH?'[22]

The editor wrote 'The Kilkenny board of guardians is the only representative body in Kilkenny where the flag of Toryism is raised triumphantly over the National banner. There is no use in concealing the fact that the board of guardians is at present in the hands of the landlords.' By bluntly stating that the landlords dominated the board of guardians he obviously feared the nationalist side would not be victorious on this occasion either. Sir Charles Wheeler Cuffe JP of Lyrath proposed the marquis of Ormonde as chairman. Simon Morris JP seconded the nomination. Tullaroan's challenger Edmond Kelly was proposed by Martin Morrissey and seconded by Daniel Quinlan of Paulstown. On a division Lord Ormonde received 19 votes and Edmond Kelly received 13. The following Saturday the *Kilkenny Journal* greeted the election with a predictable headline:

'FLUNKEYISM TRIUMPHANT!'[23]

The tone of the article ranged from acceptance to despair: 'The news that the Kilkenny flunkeys have carried the day will be received by our readers with pain, possibly with indignation but certainly not with surprise.' The editor deplored the lack of patriotism and bemoaned the fact that 'the degrading servility, which had been stamped out from almost every town and county in Ireland, reigned supreme in Kilkenny'. The reason for the defeat was summarized in this notion of servility to the gentry. It was an issue to be looked at in future if the branches were to learn any lessons from another failed attempt to unseat the marquis.

Normally the declaration of the winner in the election of chairman would mark the end of the subject until the following year. Not so on this occasion as, ironically, in October Lord Ormonde announced his intention to resign from the chairmanship because he intended leaving the country.[24] The marquis's decision seemed to catch the main players off guard although there was one letter to the *Kilkenny Journal* from a prominent nationalist, J.P. Phelan of Ballyragget, who respectfully suggested that 'the national party make another attempt to put forward a candidate who is in harmony with the popular desire.'[25] This correspondent recognized that the initiative for promoting opposition to Lord Ormonde rested with 'the patriotic people of Tullaroan'.[26] However, to the dismay of the editor of the *Kilkenny Journal* at the next board meeting the guardians voted to ask the absent marquis to reconsider his decision. Only five guardians attended and three voted to ask the marquis to change his mind. The newspaper editor despaired as he opined: 'The prospect for the future has become darker since last March and the proceedings in the board room on Thursday [28 October] affords the most incontestable proof that an honest national chairman will never sit for that union until the rate-payers take the matter into their own hands.'[27]

The following year the Tullaroan branch of the Irish National League moved much earlier on the issue and discussed it on Sunday 30 January.[28] The members decided to take the initiative and invite the branches of the Kilkenny union to meet in convention to select a nationalist candidate. In considering previous failures the apathy of some and the treachery and fear of others of the elected guardians were cited as reasons. The *Kilkenny Journal* congratulated the committee of the Tullaroan branch on their prompt and timely action. They expected that the third attempt to put a nationalist in the chair of Kilkenny union would be successful.

The convention took place at City Hall on Wednesday, 9 February 1887.[29] Ten branches were represented: Kilkenny, St Patrick's, St John's, St Canice's, Tullaroan, Ballycallan, Galmoy, Clara, Paulstown, and Freshford. The mayor of Kilkenny, P.M. Egan, chaired the meeting. After a discussion on the main issues involved, the meeting was adjourned until 19 February when every branch in the union would be asked to name its intended guardian. In every case where the intended guardian of a division failed to indicate that he would vote for the nationalist candidate, 'a suitable gentleman' would be nominated to contest the division. Nothing would be left to chance this time round.

Four days later the *Kilkenny Journal* announced in an editorial that it had learned Lord Ormonde would not contest the election. It could not resist commenting that this news had only come to light after the very successful Irish National League meeting.[30]

The reconvened meeting of the delegates from the Irish National League branches took place on Saturday, 19 February.[31] Twenty guardians promised to vote for the nationalist candidate. Nine either did not promise or did not reply. In the case of these absentees it was decided to leave it to the local branch of the League to secure their allegiance or to deal with the issue by replacing the guardian. There was also a debate on the issue of actually choosing an agreed candidate. There was a slight controversy when deciding whether the candidate would have to be an elected guardian or if a magistrate, an *ex-officio*, could be chosen. Michael Wall of Freshford said: 'There is an *ex-officio* in the parish to which I belong. He is not alone a Justice of the Peace but a member of the National League since its instigation.' The following resolution was adopted after a debate:

> That the league branches pledge the respective guardians representing them to vote for guardians as chairman, vice-chairman and deputy vice-chairman who are members of the National League and who will be selected by a majority of the elected guardians.

The delegates thus accepted that the agreed candidate could be either an *ex-officio* or an elected guardian. The meeting of the elected guardians to choose an agreed candidate took place on Wednesday 30 March 1887. This was the third centrally organized meeting to be held about the issue. Nineteen guardians attended. Four were nominated: John Francis Smithwick JP, Kilcreene Lodge, Kilkenny; James Sullivan JP, Lacken Hall, Kilkenny; Henry Berthar Loughnan JP, Crohill, Freshford, a member of the Freshford branch of the Irish National League and P.M. Egan, mayor of Kilkenny. Only one nominee, the mayor, was an elected guardian. A discussion took place as to whether Smithwick and Sullivan were willing to stand but there was no resolution proposed on the issue so it is clear that neither of them had been approached beforehand. John Francis Smithwick was chosen as the agreed nationalist candidate for the position of chairman in the election due to take place the following day. Twenty-seven guardians attended the meeting on Thursday 31 March 1887. The minutes simply record that the clerk of the union laid before the board the list of elected guardians and stated that the first business to be transacted was election of chairman. 'Mr Joseph Walsh proposed and Mr Patrick Rowan seconded that John F Smithwick Esq be elected. Agreed to unanimously.'[32] There was no further comment on the election in the minutes.

The newspaper report in the *Kilkenny Journal* two days later recorded the result under the following headline:

'UNANIMOUS ELECTION OF A NATIONALIST CHAIRMAN.'[33]

John Francis Smithwick did not attend the meeting yet he was now the new chairman of the board of guardians. John P Hyland was elected vice-chairman as in the previous year. He too was absent. Martin Morrissey was elected as deputy vice-chairman. As he was the only one of the three newly elected officers at the meeting he duly 'took the chair amidst applause'.

There was an explosive start to the new era. It will be recalled that the editor of the *Kilkenny Journal* had written in March 1886 of the immense power in the hands of all chairmen of boards of guardians when deciding what questions were suitable or unsuitable to be put before a meeting. The new board of guardians of Kilkenny poor law union did not waste time in waiting for a controversial topic to be put before deputy vice-chairman Martin Morrissey. Moments after he took the chair, the guardians launched into a debate which finished with a resolution accusing no less a person than the chief secretary of Ireland of false and untrue statements! The mayor, P.M. Egan, proposed and Edmond Walshe, the newly elected guardian for Tullaroan, seconded the following resolution, which was adopted unanimously:

That we look upon the statement of the Chief Secretary for Ireland
regarding the disorder of the country and particularly the County
Kilkenny as entirely false and untrue, that the passage of the Coercion
Act is calculated to throw this country into utter disorder and we
think it incumbent upon all honest English Liberals to oppose it to
the last extremity, as a political trick unworthy of statesmen.[34]

According to the minutes, it was ordered that the above be wired to Mr
Parnell. That too was surely a first for the Kilkenny board! This debate would
never have started under the old regime and the details must have made for
uncomfortable reading by the marquis. No doubt his morning read that distant
Saturday would have been the *Moderator*, which gave extensive coverage to
the proceedings.

That there was no air of triumph following the election is striking. One
short report in the issue of the *Journal* that followed the election was headlined:

### 'FLIGHT OF THE CONSERVATIVES'

The report simply congratulated John Smithwick on his election and noted
at the end: 'The *ex-officio* guardians, considering discretion the better part of
valour, were conspicuous by their absence.'[35] In fact the Irish National League
branches scarcely got time to savour the victory as almost immediately they
were taken up with the new coercion act, the Criminal Law and Procedure
Act (1887). This act defined intimidation and conspiracy, gave resident magistrates in districts proclaimed under the act powers of investigation and sum-
mary jurisdiction and empowered the lord lieutenant to suppress subversive
organizations.[36]

In Tullaroan the next reported meeting of the Irish National League was
devoted to protesting against the act then being debated in the house of
commons. Yet there must have been a feeling of elation amongst the members
there at their success in orchestrating the removal of the unionist marquis of
Ormonde from the chairmanship of the board of guardians, which represented the breaking of landlord domination. Over the course of the campaign,
which effectively lasted three years from the foundation of the branch, the
members learned that local government was a base for political power and
they learned how to use that power. William Feingold noted that the boards
of guardians gave tenant farmers experience of the political process within
the political system on a regular basis, providing an important preparation
for self-government.[37] The Tullaroan branch of the Irish National League
could feel rightly proud of its contribution to this national campaign but the
parishioners did not have long to wait before feeling the effects of the new
coercion act.

# 5. The 'Tullaroan Thirteen'

On Friday 24 February 1888 John Dowling, a tenant farmer from Picketstown, Tullaroan, got possession of an evicted farm of 60 acres at Knocknamuck, Tullaroan which had been vacated for over a year.[1] The landlord John St George evicted Richard Walsh from the farm in 1887. (The farm was actually situated in the townland of Adamstown.)[2] The day after Dowling took possession, the new Catholic curate of Tullaroan, the Revd John Ryan, visited him. He came to advise his parishioner not to fall out with his neighbours and to give back the farm if he did not need it. Later, Dowling also remembered meeting a neighbour Daniel Hogan of Monavedroe at that time too. Hogan threatened Dowling that if he had taken a farm from him he would very soon bring him to his knees or put him before his 'Maker'. John Dowling did not heed either the advice or the threat and held onto the farm.

On Sunday Fr Ryan said 12 o'clock Mass in Tullaroan. At the end he asked the people to stay because he had something to say to them. During mass a notice had been posted on the gate saying that a meeting of the Irish National League would be held after Mass. When Fr Ryan came out a meeting of the League was held in the grounds of the church. Fr Ryan chaired the meeting. He informed his listeners that something 'sudden had recently happened in the parish'.[3] He went on to oppose land grabbing and urge support for the rules of the League. Michael Meagher of Rathmacan endorsed Fr Ryan's words. He mentioned a case of land grabbing in Co. Tipperary where the grabber was the subject of a severe case of boycotting. James Bowe was the third speaker, claiming that 'the devil had recently come into a corner of the parish'.

A week later on Saturday, 3 March, John Dowling went to Kilkenny. Returning to Tullaroan that evening, he met two fellow parishioners, Edmond Walshe and Michael Meagher about a mile and a half from the city. They shook their whips at him and shouted and yelled until they were out of sight. Around this time too Dowling was refused sugar in a neighbouring shop and the owner of a threshing machine was warned not to employ Dowling's sister at the harvest. Dowling attended first Mass in Tullaroan the day after that unsettling experience. After the gospel Michael Meagher got up out of his seat and marched down the chapel and knelt down behind Dowling. Shortly after two stones were seen to strike Dowling on the back. Another parishioner, James Clohosey, had the poor box that day. When John Dowling put in his 'copper' Clohosey took it out and threw it on the ground. An Irish National League meeting was held immediately after Mass. The congregation waited in the chapel yard and John Dowling was subjected to a lot of shouting, jeering, and groaning as he left the church. He was followed home by some men who continued to shout and yell at him.

John Dowling had failed to realize the importance of the 'cardinal rule of the Land League' that no one should take up an evicted farm. Regarding similar incidents in Co. Cork, James S. Donnelly notes that: 'Although the weapon of the boycott was ultimately aimed at the destruction of land-lordism, its immediate targets in most instances were not the landlords or his agents.'⁴ Donnelly detailed 101 boycotting cases in Cork in 1886, which demonstrated that farmers were the most frequently censured group. In as many as 45 out of the 101 cases, those boycotted were tenants who had incurred disapproval by grabbing farms or grazing land, by paying rents or being suspected of doing so or simply by refusing to join the League.⁵

John Dowling was now suffering at the hands of the Irish National League in Tullaroan. The police took a serious view of the boycotting events that followed. Early on Monday 26 March 1888 they raided a number of homes in Tullaroan and 13 people were arrested 'on the grave charges of criminal conspiracy and unlawful assembly'.⁵ Those arrested were marched, in some cases 'with steel bracelets of rather plain workmanship on their wrists', to Tullaroan police barracks. They were Edmond Walshe, honorary secretary of the Irish National League, James Bowe, 'ex-suspect', John Dillon, Thomas Martin, John Kennedy, Michael Meagher, James Clohosey, James Kelly, John Walsh, Martin Walsh, William Walsh, Edward Quigley, and Michael Butler (aged about 14 years). They were held at the police barracks until two o'clock in the afternoon. Bail was put up by Edmond Kelly, William Dillon Snr, William Dillon Jnr, Thomas Hogan, Thomas Fleming and William Walsh. These were some of the biggest farmers in Tullaroan at that time. William Dillon Snr farmed 130 acres in the townland of Tullaroan. William Dillon Jnr was tenant on 276 acres in Ballybeagh. Thomas Hogan had 106 acres in Ballagh. Thomas Fleming held 98 acres in Monavedroe.⁶ When those who were arrested emerged from the barracks in the afternoon they were received with ringing cheers from seven or eight hundred people who marched with flags flying to a field close by where a meeting of the Irish National League was held.⁷

The *Kilkenny Journal* reporter noted the eminent position which Tullaroan had achieved in the political arena of the county by 1888 with his comment: 'There is no spot in the County Kilkenny where National politics were more heartily entered into than in Tullaroan.' The boycotted tenant received no sympathy. The reporter acknowledged that he was left entirely alone to the enjoyment of his own pleasing thoughts. In that same issue of the paper the editor explained that the ordinary course to be followed when arresting a suspect would be the issuing of summonses against the alleged offender but in this case the men were arrested under warrants and conveyed to the barracks by a strong force of constabulary. The editor stated that he had reason

15222d

to believe that these tactics were resorted to in compliance with special instructions from Dublin Castle. 'To our mind Tullaroan has reason to be proud of the distinction conferred upon it by this special mark of attention from the Coercionists,' continued the report. Unfortunately, it is not possible to confirm if in fact Dublin Castle did issue instructions for the arrests because the relevant file in the Chief Secretary's Office Registered Papers is missing.[8]

On Thursday 29 March the 'Tullaroan Thirteen' faced charges at Kilmanagh Petty sessions. Kilmanagh is approximately six miles from Tullaroan. There were 250 policemen on duty there that day, 100 from this county and 150 from Co. Tipperary, which adjoins Kilmanagh.[9] The speed with which the case and the police arrangements were carried out suggests that preparations were well advanced beforehand and indicates again that higher authorities were involved. The report of the proceedings of the trial in the *Kilkenny Journal* is headlined:

THE CRIMES ACT IN TULLAROAN.
PROCEEDINGS BEFORE THE MAGISTRATES.
Jack the Straddle on the table.
'What about the Horse Collar?'
'They looked wicked at him.'[10]

The first two headlines are self-explanatory. The next two headlines are connected to the alleged land grabber, John Dowling, and refer to an incident that occurred some time beforehand when he was accused of stealing a horse collar. This incident was alluded to during the trial. On that occasion John Dowling and his father went to Kilkenny and stabled their horse. When they came back to collect it, the collar was missing so they borrowed another one from a group of boys who were in the yard at the time. Dowling admitted that the police questioned them afterwards about the horse collar but he was adamant that he never received a summons. Because of this incident 'Jack the Straddle' was Dowling's nickname subsequently. When he explained the incident in his evidence it caused an outburst of laughter at the trial and the sub-editor obviously felt it was too good an opportunity to ignore. The last sub-headline was a quotation from Dowling's evidence when he alleged that one of the defendants had 'looked wicked at him'. If the accuser didn't feel ridiculed when the attendance in court laughed at him, then he must certainly have felt it when faced with those headlines in Saturday's newspaper. The newspaper report itself is preceded by an extraordinary preamble, which outlines in a facetious way the manner in which the apparatus of the state operated that day in Kilmanagh. The reporter knowingly adopted a stage-Irish style of writing in order to ridicule the main government representatives. 'This was a great day for the quiet little village of Kilmanagh. There were lots of "quality" out.' If people suspected they qualified under that title, they must have read on with trepidation:

There was Heffernan Considine and Johnny Bodkin and the Great Mogul Lynch, and 'Torney Watters and Barney Sheehan and Patsy Holmes and Mickey Hewitt, the three last named being all in their war paint with their ilegant [*sic*] clothes and the big soords [*sic*] by their sides, looking for all the world, like little Julius Caesars.

Heffernan Considine is listed in *Thom's directory* for 1888 as resident magistrate for Kilkenny and Joseph Lynch was resident magistrate for Castlecomer, Co. Kilkenny. Lynch had responsibility for keeping order in Kilmanagh, hence the derogatory title of 'Great Mogul'. John Bodkin is not listed in the directory but he was possibly a visiting magistrate. 'Torney Watters was Crown Solicitor Lewis James Watters Esq, AM, LLD of Dublin and Tennypark, Kilkenny who was referred to in the newspaper report of the case as Dr Watters. 'Barney' Sheehan was RIC County Inspector John Barron Sheehan, who could hardly have been impressed with the familiarity adopted by the reporter. 'Patsy' Holmes was RIC District Inspector George Holmes of the Johnstown district, which included Tullaroan. 'Mickey' Hewitt was RIC District Inspector James Malcolm Hewitt of the Callan district, which included Kilmamagh.[11] The courthouse was described as a grand building with four little windows: 'three were hermitically [*sic*] sealed, fearing a breath of fresh air might creep in and interfere with the administration of justice!'[12]

Having set the scene with this unusual depiction of what he had seen, the reporter gave a verbatim account of the proceedings of the trial. A copy of the warrant on which the men were arrested was printed the relevant section of the act under which they were charged, i.e., section 2, sub-section 1, of the Criminal Law Procedure (Ireland) Act, 1887, was quoted. Dr Watters, the crown solicitor, addressed the court and explained that all 13 of the defendants were charged with unlawful assembly and criminal conspiracy on Sunday 26 February and Sunday 4 March at Tullaroan. He outlined the events that occurred from the time Dowling took possession of the farm. The speeches that James Bowe and Michael Meagher made outside Tullaroan church on 26 February implicated them in the conspiracy. Edmond Walshe was implicated because he and Bowe indulged in threatening behaviour towards Dowling on the road from Kilkenny.

Police witnesses corroborated the prosecutor's statement that some pebbles, at least, were thrown at John Dowling at Mass on 4 March. James Clohosey's action in throwing back John Dowling's coin from the poor box caused him to be implicated in the alleged conspiracy. Dowling, gave evidence during which he implied that five more of the defendants had threatened him. On his way home from Mass on 4 March a stone was thrown at him but missed and John Kennedy, John Walsh, Martin Walsh, William Walsh and Edward Quigley then overtook him on the road, hooting and shouting.[13] These five were charged with criminal conspiracy. Of the 13 arrested for unlawful assembly, nine now faced the conspiracy charge.

The trial resumed on Tuesday 3 April 1888. The *Kilkenny Journal* reported that the village was overrun with police. The reporter was faced with his first experience of 'marshal [*sic*] law' when he tried to enter the village of Kilmanagh and his car was stopped.[14] In all probability he was the same reporter who had written in such derogatory terms the week before. He eventually gained access to the courthouse thanks to District Inspector Holmes.

Before the case for the defence was opened, the state solicitor Dr Watters announced that with regard to four of the defendants John Dillon, Thomas Martin, James Kelly and Michael Butler, no distinct overt action had been proved against them and because the evidence of their being outside the chapel on 4 March was of a more or less conflicting nature, he was satisfied, on behalf of the state, to withdraw charges against them. Edmund Leamy presented the case for the defence. In the course of his summation he observed that the land question was the cause of the misery of the people and the landlords. During the prosecutor's summing up, Dr Watters asked the magistrates 'to meet out such a punishment to the defendants as would not only be a punishment to them but a warning to others.'

The magistrates imposed a sentence of three months with hard labour on James Bowe and Michael Meagher, 'the persons who had been responsible for the unhappy conduct'. If this was because of the speeches they made at the meeting after Mass on 26 February, why was Fr Ryan not charged? After all he had chaired the meeting. Priests had been charged under the first coercion act but officialdom in Kilkenny, it seemed, was not prepared to go down that road. In the other seven cases against Clohosey, Quigley, Kennedy and the four Walshes, the magistrates failed to discover anything in their individual cases that would justify making any distinction between them. All seven were sentenced to Kilkenny gaol for one month with hard labour. Notice of appeal was granted in the case of Bowe and Meagher. They were released on bail. The charge of unlawful assembly was withdrawn. Warrants were made out for the arrest of the seven who were removed under escort from the courthouse. Outside they were greeted with loud and continuous cheers. When they arrived in Kilkenny they were met by a large number of citizens and St Patrick's brass band. The newspaper account states that, when they arrived at the gaol, the police, 'without any cause', charged the crowd: 'The attack on the people was most uncalled for and plainly shows that the authorities were only eager for an opportunity to show their prowess against unarmed citizens.'

The seven Tullaroan coercion prisoners entered Kilkenny Jail on 3 April 1888. For the next four weeks the newspaper carried reports of visits made to them by prominent people like P.M. Egan, mayor of Kilkenny, and John Smithwick JP. The mayor visited for the first time on the following morning. He found all the prisoners in their cells. Edmond Walshe PLG complained of the cold. 'The knitted gansey [*sic*] which he had brought in upon him was taken off and prison flannel substituted.'[15] The same happened to all the prisoners.

Two meetings were held in different venues on Thursday 6 April where opposition to the harsh sentence was registered. One meeting was held in Tullaroan where this reaction would have been expected but opposition to the sentence was also registered at a meeting of the board of guardians in Kilkenny, which showed how circumstances had changed there. The meeting in Tullaroan was called specially to register protest. A resolution was adopted condemning the local authorities for instigating 'such a heartless and unnecessary prosecution' and offering sympathy and support to the families of 'Balfour's prisoners'.[16] This resolution also marked a change in opinions in Tullaroan from 1881 when the first coercion prisoner, James Bowe, was forced to complain of the lack of support from his neighbours.

On Wednesday 11 April the prisoners may have thought that the hardship they were faced with was worth it because a headline in the *Kilkenny Journal* read:

'A WIN FOR THE LEAGUE.'[17]

The report stated that John Dowling had handed back the grabbed farm and that land grabbing in the parish was 'dead and buried'. However the newspaper editor was indulging in propaganda because a study of the cancelled books reveals that the opposite was the case. The cancelled books for the townland of Adamstown were revised in March 1889 and they show that John Dowling was still in possession of the farm then.[18] In August he had to receive personal protection from two constables stationed in his house at Pickettstown.[19] Oral tradition states that the ill feeling towards the Dowling family continued into the new century.[20]

On 28 March the editor of the *Kilkenny Journal* predicted in his first editorial concerning the arrests that the result would be that 'those who were luke-warm in the cause would be inspired with new spirit.' This prediction came to pass at the annual election of the Tullaroan branch of the Irish National League held on Sunday 15 April. The seven men in jail were made *ex-officio* members of the branch committee 'by the unanimous voice of the people.'[21] The sacrifice that the men were making was acknowledged by their neighbours with this gesture. The two men sentenced to three months with hard labour, James Bowe and Michael Meagher, profited by their fate as, in the election of the committee, both topped the poll with 100 votes each. The coincidence of both getting the exact same high number of votes suggests vote managing of the highest order or, more likely, that the controllers of the vote did not wish to display favouritism to either one. The total number of votes cast at the meeting came to 635, which was indeed an extraordinary turnout. An addendum to the report of this meeting informs readers that during the previous week a number of farmers, with their men and horses, assembled on the farms of Edmond Walshe and James Clohosey to set the potato and oat crops: 'The progress made through the work by the willing hands was truly astonishing – each man vying [*sic*] with his neighbour for superiority in the handling of the plough and the wielding of the manure sprong.'[22] James Bowe must have looked on this work with a wry smile as he recalled the autumn of 1881 when he was a prisoner under the first coercion act and his family depended on his neighbours from the next parish to help save the crops. The reaction of the community in Tullaroan had changed much in seven years. At the onset of the sowing season in 1888, as seven men faced a month in prison, the concerns of their families must have been added to by fear for their crops but neighbourly co-operation within the community came to their rescue. This time the sacrifice was recognized.

Having served the full sentence, the prisoners were released on Monday 30 April.[23] They were met at the prison gates by a number of their friends from Tullaroan and were escorted through the city by St Patrick's brass band. During the morning large numbers of supporters of the Irish National League had arrived from neighbouring parishes to take part in the procession to Tullaroan. A public meeting was held on the Parade (the public square) in Kilkenny. It was addressed by the mayor, P.M. Egan. He congratulated 'the brave men of Tullaroan' and said they had suffered 'for one of the principles which every Irishman was prepared to suffer, the principles of the League – that no man should take a farm from which another was unduly evicted'. Two of the former prisoners, Edmond Walshe and James Clohosey, addressed the meeting on behalf of the prisoners and thanked the mayor and the other gentlemen who had visited them in prison. After the speeches, the procession moved up High Street and set out for Tullaroan. When they arrived there, 'a most hearty reception' was extended to them. All the surrounding hills were ablaze with bonfires and the houses in the village were illuminated. The *Journal* editor noted that the demonstration witnessed in Kilkenny that day proved the absurdity of supposing that imprisonment could have any effect in preventing the Irish people from 'acting up to the spirit and letter of the National League teaching'. At the next meeting of the Tullaroan branch of the Irish National League there was an understandable air of triumph as the prisoners were congratulated on their release: 'If [Chief Secretary] Balfour meant to strike terror in Kilkenny, he came to the wrong place when he selected Tullaroan. As well now as in the brave days of old, Tullaroan men were not afraid to stand in the gap of danger'.[24] These comments give an indication of the pride felt in the parish at the sacrifice endured by the men. In fact it was the ladies of Tullaroan who first alluded to the honour of the parish when they convened a meeting at the end of April to show solidarity ✓ with the prisoners. At that meeting it was resolved 'that a fund be started so that no expense should fall on any of the brave men who were made to suffer for upholding and sustaining the honour of the parish at this crisis in the history of our dear, unfortunate country'.[25] To administer the above fund the officers of the old Ladies' Land League were unanimously called upon to

take up their positions of president, treasurer, secretary and committee. The
resurrection of the Ladies' Land League was another consequence of the
coercion arrests in Tullaroan. In this it was different if not unique from the
national trend because after the demise of the Ladies' Land League in 1884
the organization did not, or was not allowed to, reappear on the national scene.
Michael Meagher proposed a special vote of thanks to the ladies of Tullaroan
at the Irish National League meeting in May and it was passed by acclamation.

The appeal by James Bowe and Michael Meagher against the sentence of
three months with hard labour was heard on Thursday 7 June at the Kilkenny
quarter sessions. There was no new evidence submitted. The sentence was
confirmed and Bowe and Meagher were taken into custody to Kilkenny jail
escorted by a large crowd of supporters. The prisoners were visited the following day by the mayor who reported that 'the probable cutting of their whiskers
is a humiliation they could be well spared'.[26] From the time he entered prison
on 7 June, James Bowe refused to take outdoor exercise as a protest against
doing so in company with the ordinary criminals in jail. The mayor reported to
the prison board that there was plenty of vacant space in the yard where the
prisoners could exercise by themselves. He asked that permission be granted to
them to do so but it was refused. James Bowe in turn refused to take the
exercise and he was sentenced to 24 hours with bread and water. When the
mayor visited them on 19 June he found both prisoners in the exercise yard. It
is not clear whether they were with the 'ordinary' criminals or not. Later in his
sentence James Bowe suffered from ill health, which probably forced him to
adopt a more conciliatory attitude, but he had made his point. He believed
that he was a political prisoner and merited special status.

As the release of the prisoners was anticipated in the final week of August,
the editor of the *Journal* considered the agricultural outlook in the county.
He believed the year would be disastrous for the Irish farmer.[27] Heavy rain
that week did irreparable damage to the crops but the release of the
prisoners lifted the gloom. The editor noted that they would be returning to
active political life once more.[28] The prisoners were released at 7.30 a.m. on
Wednesday 29 August.[29] An immense crowd of friends and sympathisers
from their own district and the city attended, accompanied by St Patrick's
brass band. They proceeded to Mrs Hackett's, Walkin Street where they had a
substantial breakfast. Afterwards they made their way to the Parade for a
public meeting. The mayor addressed the meeting first and expressed the same
sentiments that he had spoken in May when the first group of prisoners were
released. Michael Meagher stood to speak and was greeted with cries of
'Bold Tullaroan'. He noted that neither he nor his friend Mr Bowe imagined
that the meeting had been called simply for their sakes. They looked upon it
as a protest against Mr Balfour for his infamous coercion act. James Bowe also
spoke and was received with 'cheers, again and again renewed'. He showed that
he was a student of history when alluding to the Liberator. He told his listeners

that when the Liberator wanted to rivet the attention of his audience, he referred to dates 'for instance, it was the 23 August 1172 when the first Saxon foot pressed the soil of Ireland and cursed be that day in the memory of every Irishman'. The latter half of the quotation may have been Bowe's own embellishment, which invoked cheers from the crowd. Then he told his listeners that he had his own important dates: 'It was on 24 February 1888 that the first evicted farm was taken in his native parish … and the 26 March [when the 13 were arrested] was the greatest day for the National League they ever had in Tullaroan.' This statement reveals as much about the character of James Bowe as any we have come across since he first came to prominence back in 1881. Arrest and imprisonment were of greater import to him than the success that the Tullaroan National League had achieved in the board of guardians elections the year before. For all his acceptance of the constitutional route to political change since his first prison term in 1881, James Bowe retained his militancy throughout.

After the speeches, about 50 cars formed a procession to take the released men home. By the time it reached Tullaroan, the procession 'fully covered an Irish mile of the way.' This too marked a significant change from the position in 1881 when James Bowe returned from Naas Jail. It will be recalled that on that occasion the band failed to appear to welcome him home because the then curate, the Revd Patrick Meany, had requested them not to. Now the vice-president of the Irish National League, the Revd John Ryan CC presided at the reception in the village. It is noteworthy that when the prisoners were released at the beginning of May and at the end of August no opportunity was lost by any of the speakers at the public gatherings to refer to the principle for which the men had been imprisoned, that is, that no man should take a farm from which another had been unduly evicted. The hardships endured by the prisoners were severe but they did not change their opinions. As James Bowe stated on the day of his release: 'Mr Balfour and his accomplices were so blind to think the principles inculcated by Mr Davitt can be blotted out by the prison.'

In March 1888 a *Kilkenny Journal* reporter remarked on Tullaroan's eminent position in political circles in Kilkenny. No doubt having its own 'felons' added to its status. The Irish National League branch in Tullaroan continued to lead from the front. In the spring of 1889 the branch took the initiative in calling a meeting of branches from surrounding parishes to consider some local issues. This meeting took place on 17 March 1889 in Tullaroan. The meeting was judged to be a complete success: 'The usual fault of such assemblies – too much talk – was quite absent.'[30] A resolution was adopted renewing the delegates' confidence in their 'illustrious' leader Charles Stewart Parnell and congratulating him on his triumph over the conspiracy got up by the wretched *Times*. This open display of support for Parnell contrasted with feelings within the Irish Party later that year. In May William O'Brien MP secured Parnell's support for an appeal for funds to support the plan of campaign, a new strategy to withhold rent. On 11 July 1889 the *Freeman's Journal* announced, on Parnell's authority, the immediate formation of a tenants' association 'to counteract the landlord combination'. It was very slow to get off the ground because, wrote William O'Brien, 'Parnell will not do anything himself'.[31] Eventually the new league, called the Irish Tenants' Defence Association was launched at a meeting of the Irish Party in the Mansion House on 24 October 1889. The first convention was held in Thurles, Co. Tipperary, on 28 October. A convention was held at Kilkenny on 13 November. Edmond Walshe, Henry J. Meagher, Michael Meagher and John Doheny represented Tullaroan.[32] John Doheny was a new member of the Irish National League committee. He was tenant on 72 acres in the townland of Tullaroan. Parnell did not attend the Thurles convention but he had covered his absence by writing an open letter saying that the state of his health would prevent him from attending.[33] Laurence Geary comments that Parnell's absence from the Thurles convention gave rise to a great deal of scepticism. The storm clouds were gathering concerning his relationship with Mrs Katherine O'Shea but that would not have been the feeling amongst the tenants especially as the Tenants Defence Association gave new life to the agrarian dispute.

The unexpected death in September 1890 of the North Kilkenny MP, Edward Mulhallen Marum, left a vacancy in Westminster. After a suitable period of mourning, Edmond Walshe, secretary of the Tullaroan branch of the Irish National League, wrote a letter to the *Kilkenny Journal* calling on the constituents of North Kilkenny to think of choosing a successor to the

late Mr Marum.[34] He may not have been aware of the fact but two days before his letter was printed in the *Journal* the London Divorce Court delivered its verdict in a case where the leader of the Irish Parliamentary Party, Charles Stewart Parnell, had been named as co-respondent. The verdict would have far reaching consequences, even in remote Tullaroan.

*3* Edmond Walshe, secretary of Tullaroan Irish National League; sentenced to one month with hard labour in Kilkenny Jail, 4 April–30 April 1888.
*Source:* Mrs Celia Kennedy, Ballylarkin, Freshford, grand-daughter of Edmond Walshe.

# 6. The impact of the Parnell Split on Tullaroan

The romance between Charles Stewart Parnell and Mrs Katherine O'Shea, wife of Captain William O'Shea, has been described as 'the great love affair of the Victorian age.'[1] The couple met for the first time on 30 July 1880 and the affair lasted until Parnell's death in October 1891. It was well known in political circles that the relationship existed but it did not interfere with Parnell's career until Captain O'Shea filed for divorce in December 1889. If anyone amongst the general public was unaware of the relationship, it was confirmed for everyone when Parnell issued a public statement after the application for divorce was made to the court. This statement revealed clearly that there was a basis to the charge of adultery. Parnell seems to have hoped that, while the charge of adultery was not false, because he had followed a gentleman's code of honour and Captain O'Shea had not been deceived, he would not be harshly judged. Paul Bew states that this explains Parnell's assurance to Michael Davitt that 'he would emerge from the whole trouble without a stain on his reputation'.[2] However, that was not how things turned out but a year passed before the divorce case was heard in London.

During 1890, the Tullaroan branch of the Irish National League was taken up with usual matters. On New Year's Day, the branch condemned, in a newspaper report, the sittings of the Land Commission in Kilkenny and elsewhere as a 'mockery, a delusion and a snare to the tenant farmers of the county.'[3] The branch recommended that all tenants still fortunate not to have had their cases heard by the commission should seriously consider withdrawing from the commission while they still had time because the reductions given by the court were 'ridiculously and shamefully inadequate'.

In July the Tullaroan branch communicated with the neighbouring branch in Kilmanagh to encourage the members there to ensure that anyone requiring grass for meadowing should prove their nationalist credentials by dealing with nationalists only.[4] There is no evidence to show that this was what was happening in Tullaroan but presumably it was. The report of the Kilmanagh meeting notes that their members were very pleased at having the matter brought to their attention by their neighbours, which showed that Tullaroan's leadership role was still vital in the locality. Who could have foreseen then the division that was about to overtake the Irish National League?

The date for the by-election to fill the vacancy at Westminster caused by the death of Edward Mulhallen Marum was set for 20 December 1890. The events surrounding the by-election campaign cannot be separated from the fallout surrounding the O'Shea divorce case. The fact that the election campaign coincided with the fallout meant that crucial developments occurred in both Kilkenny and London almost simultaneously. The by-election in North Kilkenny became the first test of Charles Stewart Parnell's position at home after the divorce case was made public. The divorce case began in London on 15 November 1890. No defence was entered and the case lasted a mere two days. A *decree nisi* was granted on 17 November. In Kilkenny the subsequent editorial in the *Kilkenny Journal* noted that the anti-Irish newspapers were 'shrieking with savage and unrestrained delight' over the case.[5] The *Journal* itself had no desire 'to palliate or excuse Mr Parnell' but it would be 'neither his judges nor his keepers and with his private life it is not the province of the public to interfere'. In this same 19 November issue of the paper the Tullaroan branch of the Irish National League brought the issue of the by-election to the fore.

The branch held a meeting on Friday 14 November and a report was printed in the *Kilkenny Journal* on the following Wednesday. The members passed a resolution which deemed it expedient that the branches of the Irish National League in North Kilkenny should meet in convention for the purpose of selecting a candidate, for the forthcoming by-election, who would have Mr Parnell's approval. The branch begged leave to take the initiative in 'this most important matter' and hoped that the league branches of the county would not consider their action 'dictatorial'.[6] This was an unusual intervention into the preliminaries of an election as the Irish Parliamentary Party usually chose an election candidate. The Tullaroan Irish National League branch was effectively attempting to nominate its own candidate, hoping that the Party, and more particularly Parnell, would row in with approval subsequently. Circulars were sent to the branches in North Kilkenny announcing the convention and a copy was printed in that edition of the paper under the report of the meeting. Unusual as this intervention was, it was typical of the Tullaroan branch and was consistent with the other occasions in recent years when it had chosen to take the initiative but a new dimension was added to Tullaroan's involvement in the by-election by a third piece of correspondence, a letter, also published in this issue of the *Journal*. This time the Tullaroan correspondent may have gone a step too far. The letter was written by one of the branch secretaries, Edmond Walshe, who went so far as to suggest his own nominee, Gerald Brennan, a magistrate from Eden Hall, Ballyragget, for the vacant seat at Westminster. By so doing he went even further than his colleagues at the branch meeting. He appealed to the pride of the people when he said that it would be 'a blow to our prestige if it could be said that, at this important moment of our country's fortunes, there were none amongst us able and willing to do battle on behalf of the county.'[7] He also made a remarkable claim that in all probability this would be the last contest that would ever take place for the representation of North Kilkenny in the British house of commons.

The convention called by the Tullaroan Irish National League was due to take place on Monday 24 November. The people of Tullaroan and North Kilkenny may not have been aware but important meetings were also taking place in London at this time. Parliament was due to reconvene on 25 November. The Irish Parliamentary Party was also due to meet that day to elect its sessional leader. Before this meeting took place the leader of the Liberal Party, William Gladstone, made it clear to Justin McCarthy, who was, effectively, Parnell's deputy, that, because of the circumstances in which Parnell found himself, the Liberals could no longer support an alliance with the Irish Party if Parnell continued as leader. This added to the significance of the upcoming meeting of the Irish Parliamentary Party.

It is unclear whether the Irish Party was aware of the proposed convention to select a local candidate due to be held in Kilkenny on Monday 24 November. It was surely more than a coincidence when events occurred on Sunday 23 November that negated Tullaroan's call for a convention and rendered all the correspondence about a local candidate irrelevant. Cornelius J. Kenealy, town clerk of Kilkenny, who was also editor of the *Kilkenny Journal*, received a request that day from the joint secretaries of the Irish Tenants' Defence Association to organize a convention, for Thursday 27 November, the purpose of which was 'to forward the objects of the association.'[8] The secretaries were, of course, all sitting MPs and members of the Irish Parliamentary Party. The fact that Kenealy was contacted on the Sabbath day indicates that there was a sense of urgency about the Tenants' Association call, that is, to stop the locally organized meeting, due to be held the following day. The loose description of the purpose of the meeting also indicates that there was more to it than simply wanting 'to forward the objects of the association'. Nothing further was heard of Gerald Brennan or of the idea of a local candidate. The new convention provided an opportunity for the Irish Party candidate, the Cork man Sir John Pope Hennessy, whose selection was announced in the paper on Wednesday 26 November, to be introduced to his constituents for the first time.

Meanwhile the meeting to elect the sessional leader of the Irish Parliamentary Party took place in Westminster on 25 November. Justin McCrathy attempted to contact Parnell with the important message from Gladstone outlining the concerns of the Liberal Party about their future relationship with the Irish Party if Parnell continued as leader. McCarthy either failed to deliver the message or else he failed to make an impact on Parnell. More importantly, he also failed to tell the other party members once the meeting had started. When it came to a vote Parnell was unanimously re-elected to the chair in spite of the fact that some members had gone to the meeting expecting him to resign. The fallout from this meeting began immediately. When it became clear that the Irish Party had been left in the dark concerning the Liberals, Gladstone published the details immediately in a letter to the *Times*. This resulted in 31 members of the Irish Party signing a requisition for another special meeting. It was now clear that the crisis was not going to go away.

At Kilkenny in accordance with the circular issued by Cornelius J. Kenealy, Town Clerk, as directed by the council of the Tenants' Defence Association, delegates from 31 branches of the Irish National League attended a convention held in the Town Hall on Thursday 27 November 1890.[9] Edmond Walshe, Henry J. Meagher, James Tone, William Hogan, Thomas Martin and James Clohosey represented Tullaroan. There was a large number of clergy present also though the editor of the *Kilkenny Journal* noted the 'undefined position of the clergy' regarding the unsettled political affairs when he commented on the convention the following Saturday.

John Redmond MP chaired the convention. He advised against mentioning the national crisis at all. Perhaps this was the reason that Tullaroan's proposed convention was superseded; the leaders of the Irish Party did not trust the local leaders to organize the convention without alluding to, and, perhaps, falling victim to the fallout from the controversy. A united front was demonstrated when it came to nominating the candidate for the by-election. The Revd Nicholas Murphy PP of Kilmanagh and Edmond Walshe of Tullaroan joined forces, the former proposing John Pope Hennessy as the candidate to represent North Kilkenny and the latter seconding the resolution. The choice of the Tullaroan man to second the resolution was probably in deference to the efforts of that branch to organize the earlier convention and showed that the Irish Party could be diplomatic at least in spite of its difficulties.

The report of the events in Saturday's *Kilkenny Journal* gives the impression of an upbeat mood. The editorial in the same issue was different. The editor had the benefit of knowing of the developments regarding Gladstone's letter to the Irish Party and he warned:

> The clouds are gathering faster and faster, the gloom is deepening and the nation – appalled by the gravity of the crisis – stands dazed, paralysed and disheartened, waiting for the storm to pass over harmlessly, or to burst with devastating effect upon the land.[10]

Despair was setting in but Parnell was still written of in affectionate and sympathetic terms. He was to the Irish people 'the same hero that the FIRST NAPOLEON was to the OLD GUARD.' The editor wrote of the pity and grief that the Irish people felt for Parnell but he also warned: 'There is one [sacrifice] which they will not make and let us trust the God of Nations may spare our country the pain of adding one pang to the sufferings of the Irish leader'.

At Westminster 74 MPs attended the Irish Party meeting on Monday 1 December 1890.[11] As the Wednesday edition of the *Kilkenny Journal* went to press the debate was still going on at Westminster but it was clear enough to the newspaper editor that the Irish Party was heading for division. This edition of the newspaper also carried a copy of a telegram sent by Archbishop Croke of Cashel to Justin McCarthy, vice-chairman of the Irish Parliamentary Party, in which he set out his position regarding the affair. He expressed sorrow for Parnell but called for his retirement. The *Journal* editor referred to this and asked:

> 'Are we to find internal strife once more raging through the land? To find Mr Parnell and his following ... on one side and Archbishops Walshe and Croke and a large circle of Irish representatives on the other. God forbid that it should come to that.'[12]

That is indeed what happened because on that very day, Wednesday 3 December, the Catholic hierarchy, with the support of the majority of the priests called on the Catholic people of Ireland to repudiate Parnell. This decision coincided with the announcement of the outcome of the Irish Party meeting in Westminster. As that meeting came to a close the majority of the party – 45 members, led by Justin McCarthy – withdrew from Committee Room Fifteen, leaving Parnell with 27 followers. The position was finally clear. The Irish Party was divided. The *Kilkenny Journal* appealed for patience and 'a little forbearing' and congratulated the county and city of Kilkenny where 'there has been no inclination to rush prematurely at con- clusions, to separate into factions which militate seriously against our united actions in the future.'[13] Such a magnanimous position would indeed have been praiseworthy if it were correct but on Thursday 4 December, two days before the newspaper was published, St Patrick's branch of the Irish National League declared that 'the leadership of Mr Parnell is now impossible.'[14] On the same day Galmoy branch declared that Mr Parnell was unfit to be leader. Two days later the priests of Kilkenny city stated that Parnell's bid to hold onto the leadership would be injurious to the home rule cause. When news of these decisions became public the following week, the editor of the *Kilkenny Journal* eventually made up his mind and got off the fence. In a dramatic opening to his editorial in the midweek edition he stated:

> The issue is knit. The battle has opened all along the line and once more the sound of angry party cries is heard in our own ranks. Poor Ireland! Surely is she 'the most distressful country that ever yet was seen'.[15]

The editorial drew attention to the fact that up to then the paper had avoided writing anything about the crisis that would have incited bitterness but the road was now divided and 'we must elect which we shall walk in future'.

The about-turn adopted by the *Kilkenny Journal* regarding Parnell and his followers in this issue of the paper was nearly as spectacular as the fall of Parnell itself. The editor noted that the bishops had solemnly declared that

Parnell could no longer lead the Irish nation. Readers were informed that Parnell had arrived in Ireland and he had come 'to invite Catholic Ireland to give the Bishops the lie'. As far as the editor was concerned this was a step too far. He immediately introduced a note of venom to the proceedings with his comment: 'The idea of trying to induce them [the Irish people] to push aside the Irish Hierarchy and Clergy at the bidding of a Protestant is too wild to be seriously entertained.' When it comes to understanding why the *Kilkenny Journal* eventually took such a strong stand against Parnell, it can be traced directly to the intervention of the bishops. Marie-Louise Legg has written that the paper changed tactics, putting the emphasis on measures, not men. 'Ireland was the issue not men's fickle adherence to party'.[16] Yet, in order to follow this course, the newspaper focussed on the 'dastardly conduct' of one man – Parnell.[17]

On Thursday 11 December the priests of the northern and city deaneries of the diocese of Ossory met in Kilkenny city and in Ballyragget. The priests in both venues pledged themselves to support Justin McCarthy and the majority of the Irish Party, rather than recognize the faction led by a man 'convicted and befouled by reason of the decision of the London Divorce Court.'[18] By now Parnell's by-election candidate, John Pope Hennessy, had also announced that he too would 'heartily welcome the advice of our Bishops and Clergy on questions affecting the welfare of Ireland.'[19] This decision placed him in opposition to Parnell and forced the latter to choose another candidate for the by-election.

The by-election campaign opened on Thursday 11 December 1890 with the arrival of members of the Irish Parliamentary Party in Kilkenny. Pierce Mahony MP and John Pope Hennessy arrived on the afternoon train. Pierce Mahony addressed the large crowd that gathered to meet the train. He announced that Mr Parnell had selected Vincent Scully of Mantle Hill, Co. Tipperary, as the candidate for North Kilkenny. This announcement must have raised eyebrows generally in the constituency and specifically in Tullaroan. If ever there was a time for a local candidate, surely this was it. Perhaps the strength of the division in the ranks was not yet obvious but whatever hope Parnell entertained of victory in the election having a local candidate would at least have provided a base from which to start. In Tullaroan the announcement must have caused a commotion too when the electors of that parish realized that if they were to stay loyal to Parnell they would have to vote for a member of the Scully family. Vincent Scully was a nephew of William Scully who had a notorious reputation as a landlord in Ireland and especially in Tullaroan. Vincent Scully's father, also Vincent, had been an MP for Co. Cork, 1852–57 and 1859–65.[20] He arrived in Kilkenny later that Thursday evening accompanied by William Redmond MP and James Dalton MP. They were greeted by a large crowd and escorted to the Victoria Hotel accompanied by torchbearers and a band.

Michael Davitt arrived in Kilkenny on the midday train on Friday 12 December. His reception committee consisted of a number of priests, one town commissioner, the candidate John Pope Hennessy and his election agent Michael Murphy, a Kilkenny solicitor. They conferred with Davitt at the Imperial Hotel and a meeting was arranged for the Town Hall later that evening to support Hennessy's candidature. At that meeting Davitt stated that he would fight the cause of Ireland against any man no matter what his name or record. As far as he was concerned the issue in the election was not between Sir John Pope Hennessy or Vincent Scully but between Ireland and an 'Insulting Dictator.'[21] This demonstrates the extent of the divide that existed between the two former allies, Davitt and Parnell. Davitt went so far as to pronounce that it was their duty 'to crush him [Parnell] at the polls'. It must have pained Parnell to hear Davitt speak of the necessity of recording a vote for the national honour against 'a man who was preparing to trample the character of the Celtic race into the dust'. Such bitterness indicates the extent to which Parnell's enemies were prepared to go to end his career as leader of the Irish Parliamentary Party.

Charles Stewart Parnell arrived in Kilkenny on the late evening train on Friday 12 December. A large crowd greeted him too, though there were no priests named in the welcoming party. He was brought to the Victoria Hotel, led by a torchlight procession that included three bands. The horses were removed from under his cab and it was drawn through John Street by the people. On his arrival at the hotel, speeches were delivered from one of the hotel windows while a number of his followers waited inside in the room. These followers included Edmond Walshe of Tullaroan who addressed the crowd from the hotel window. He said he was proud to stand there that night in support of Mr Parnell. The fact that he was a member of the welcoming party is an indication of the stature that Edmond Walshe possessed at this time in the Parnell camp in Kilkenny. The election campaign continued over the following days. On Sunday 14 December Parnell was brought through north-west Kilkenny. He spoke at Callan and Kilmanagh and from there went on to Tullaroan. He addressed a meeting there but is not quoted in any of the newspapers.[22] It can be assumed that Edmond Walshe would have had a prominent role to play at that meeting.

Oral tradition states that Parnell visited the Walshe family home that day in order to show appreciation for Edmond Walshe's support.[23] While there he presented three bronze medals to Edmond's three daughters Celia, Ann and Dorothy. Dorothy was Dick Walshe's mother. In 1910 she married her namesake, Laurence Walshe and their son Dick is now the proud owner of her medal (fig. 4). The other medals are still in the possession of the families of the other two sisters. The medal is approximately the size of a two-euro coin. The front bears a profile of Parnell's head surrounded by the inscription: '1891 Ireland's Army of Independence'. A wreath of ivy and shamrock leaves

4 Medal presented, according to oral tradition, by Charles Stewart Parnell to the Walshe family, The Church, Tullaroan, 14 December 1890.
*Source:* Mr Dick Walshe, The Church, Tullaroan, grandson of Edmond Walshe.

surrounds this. On the back of the medal is the inscription: 'Let my love be conveyed to my colleagues and the Irish people.' In 1991 the three medals were brought together again in the Walshe family home in Tullaroan by the cousins at a family reunion. The original Walshe family home is now derelict. When a new dwelling house was built in 1974 care was taken to transfer the fireplace from the parlour of the old house to the sitting room in the new house because 'Charles Stewart Parnell was entertained while sitting there.' Despite efforts to confirm the date when these medals were manufactured, it has not been possible to do so. If Parnell and his followers believed that the 'Army of Independence' would indeed deliver on its promise in the new year, the North Kilkenny by-election campaign showed that it was a divided 'Army'.

Monday 15 December was the last day for nominations of candidates to be handed into City Hall for the forthcoming election. Nine nomination papers were received for Vincent Scully as opposed to five for John Pope Hennessy;[24] 26 men from Tullaroan signed the nomination papers for Scully while two Tullaroan men signed Hennessy's papers (Table 4). This was an extraordinarily public display of support by these men for Parnell and his candidate in the context of the call by the bishops and the majority of the clergy to repudiate him.

The election took place on Monday 22 December. It was believed that there would be a full turnout of the electors but that was not the case. Out of a possible 5,790 voters, 3,972 (68.6 per cent) went to the poll.[25] The votes were counted on Tuesday and the result was announced at three o'clock in the afternoon. The result was Sir John Pope Hennessy 2,527 (63.6 per cent); Mr Vincent Scully 1,365 (34.4 per cent). The majority was 1,162. Oral tradition

**Table 4. Nominators from Tullaroan of North Kilkenny
by-election candidates, 15 December 1890**

| Nominator | Address | Nominator | Address |
|---|---|---|---|
| **Candidate: Vincent Scully (Parnellite)** | | | |
| John Walton | Remeen | John Dowling | Rathealy |
| John Reilly | Huntstown | P Grace | Trenchardstown |
| Lacton Hoyne | Lissballyfroot | Dr M A Warren | Tullaroan |
| William Walsh | Tullaroan | Columb Kennedy | Adamstown |
| William Dillon | Tullaroan | William Kavanagh | Ballybeagh |
| James Grace | Brittas | William Young | Brabstown |
| James J Neill | Courtstown | William Kavanagh | Ballybeagh |
| Patrick Grace | Ballyroe | John Maher | Foyletaylor |
| Michael Meagher | Rathmacan | Michael Maher | Rathmacan |
| James Bowe | Huntstown | John O'Neill | Canvarstown |
| Daniel Grace | Gaulstown | William Gaffney | Remeen |
| Daniel Kerwick | Huntstown | Edmond Walshe | Huntstown |
| James Hogan | Gaulstown | Richard Ryan | Foyletaylor |
| **Candidate: Sir John Pope Hennessy (Anti-Parnellite)** | | | |
| James Clohosey | Tullaroan | Thomas Martin | Tullaroan |

*Source: Kilkenny Journal* 17 December 1890.

states that the students in the diocesan seminary at St Kieran's College were given early Christmas leave in order to return home to exhort their families and neighbours not to vote for Parnell's candidate.[26] True or false, Parnell's first direct appeal to a body of Irish electors was rejected by a majority of almost two to one.

It was felt in Kilkenny that the by-election result had settled Parnell's fate so far as his position in Irish politics was concerned.[27] In hindsight this was a correct reading of the position but into the new year he clung on to the leadership of the party or his faction of it at any rate. In February 1891 the *Kilkenny Journal* once again called for his retirement. In mid-February the paper published the full Lenten pastoral of the bishop of Ossory, Abraham Brownrigg.[28] While exhorting his flock to fast during the holy season the bishop informed them that the great fast required of them was the fast from sin and especially from the sin of intemperance and impurity. Regarding the latter the bishop stated that no vice had been visited with such public and terrible chastisements from heaven as impurity. Of course the bishop was presented at that moment with a ready-made example of such public chastisement in the state of 'our own poor country'. The editor of the *Journal* was particularly impressed by the pastoral because it showed the bishop wished not merely to protect the spiritual interests of his flock but 'to guard against their being ensnared by the wiles of undesigning politicians.' How long could Parnell's supporters in north Kilkenny go on in the wake of these sentiments? To add to their woes a new national organisation, the Irish National Federation, was founded on 10 March 1891. *Kilkenny Journal* readers were informed that it would take the place of the Irish National League, which was described as the organisation which Mr Balfour tried in vain to kill but which Mr Parnell had 'effectually crippled and rendered useless.'[29]

Not everybody shared the opinions of the bishop of Ossory and the *Kilkenny Journal.* A Parnell Leadership Committee was formed in Kilkenny on Wednesday 11 February, the very day that the bishop's pastoral was published. On the committee were Edmond Walshe and Dr Michael A. Warren of Tullaroan.

The board of guardians' elections were held in March 1891. Twenty-five of the guardians were returned unopposed. Three of the electoral divisions, which had a contest, were in Tullaroan. In each of them a Parnellite candidate stood against an anti-Parnellite. This demonstrated extraordinary adherence to principles by both sides. In Ballinamara Nicholas Grace (anti-Parnellite) defeated Thomas Hogan (Parnellite) by 80 (61.6 per cent) votes to 50 (38.4 per cent). In Rathealy John Neary (anti-Parnellite) defeated Daniel Hogan (Parnellite) by 63 (71.6 per cent) votes to 25 (28.4 per cent). In the DED of Tullaroan James Bowe (Parnellite) was nominated to contest the election against John Doheny (anti-Parnellite). Bowe lodged an objection to Doheny on the grounds that the latter could not nominate himself. The clerk upheld the objection and James Bowe was deemed to be elected. Even without an election, this was the high point of James Bowe's public career. He was the only Parnellite returned in the four divisions where an election had taken place.

Throughout 1891 Parnell's physical deterioration was obvious to all. He died at his home shortly after midnight on Tuesday 6 October 1891. The death took place too late to be reported in the *Kilkenny Journal* the day after but it was the subject of an editorial the following Saturday. The paper acknowledged that Ireland would be 'a recreant nation if she did not mourn over the grave of the great Tribune she was proud to call her son.'[30] Tellingly, no black mourning bands separated the columns of print on the pages of the *Kilkenny Journal* as had been done to mark the passing of Joseph Biggar, A.M. Sullivan, Edward Mulhallen Marum and other prominent nationalists in recent years. Ironically, the death of Sir John Pope Hennessy was also reported in that issue of the paper. He died the day after Parnell. No black mourning bands were used for this report either but the obituary took up nearly two full columns of the paper. Editorial comment on Parnell's death measured scarcely half a column.

The first reported meeting of the Tullaroan branch of the Irish National League in 1891 took place on 4 January when a vote of sympathy was passed with Edmond Walshe following the death of his mother. He was not at the meeting but this may have been because of the family bereavement. The fact that he was still referred to as 'our secretary' suggests that all was well in the branch. In addition the presence at the meeting of James Bowe and the other joint secretary of the branch Henry J. Meagher also indicates that the ranks were not yet divided. However, within a few weeks a split became apparent when James Bowe opposed John Doheny, a fellow Irish National League committee member, in the Kilkenny poor law union election already alluded to. Some few weeks later in May both James Bowe and Henry J Meagher attended the previously mentioned Parnell Leadership Committee meeting in Kilkenny.

The fact that there were no reports of branch meetings held in Tullaroan during the by-election campaign hints that, in spite of appearances, all may not have been well. It is difficult to believe that Edmond Walshe, as branch secretary, would not have wanted to show his support for Parnell in a practical way at a branch meeting. However, that he did not do this indicates that he encountered opposition on a scale sufficient to prevent him calling a meeting. Of course the parish priest, Fr Jeremiah Downey, who was president of the Irish National League branch in Tullaroan, had shown which side he was on when he attended the city deanery meeting in Kilkenny on 11 December where Parnell had been condemned. He was hardly going to facilitate the calling of a meeting by his errant secretary. Eventually the catalyst for the split to become public was the poor law union election.

The founding of the new anti-Parnellite national organization, the Irish National Federation, on 10 March 1891 in Dublin added further to the division in the country. In Tullaroan a branch of the new organization was formed on 7 June 1891.[31] The membership of the committee of the new organisation can be compared with the membership of the Irish National League committee, which met on 4 January (Table 5).

The new organisation was launched in Tullaroan without Edmond Walshe, James Bowe or Henry J. Meagher. Apart from these, it can be seen from the comparison that the Irish National League committee membership transferred practically en masse to the new Irish National Federation. In that context Walshe, Bowe and Meagher displayed commendable courage in standing by the beleaguered Irish Party leader in spite of the numbers lined up on the other side. Of the 26 men who signed Parnellite Vincent Scully's nomination papers prior to the by-election the previous December (Table 4), only two, William Walsh and William Dillon, publicly switched sides to sit on the Irish National Federation committee. Of the remaining 24, James Bowe, Edmond Walshe and Dr Michael Warren, publicly supported Parnell. The affiliation of the remaining 21 nominators is not clear. The two men who signed John Pope

### Table 5. Membership of the INL and the INF committees in Tullaroan in 1891

| INL meeting, 4 January 1891 | INF meeting, 7 June 1891 |
| --- | --- |
| Revd Jeremiah Downey PP, chairman | Revd Jeremiah Downey PP, chairman. |
| Revd John Ryan CC, vice-chairman | Revd John Ryan CC, vice-chairman |
| Henry J Meagher, hon. sec. | Timothy Kelly, hon. sec. |
| Edmond Walshe, hon. sec. | John Morris, hon. sec. |
| John Doheny, treasurer | John Doheny, treasurer |
| Michael Ryan | Nicholas Grace, treasurer |
| Patrick Delaney | Patrick Delaney |
| William Dillon | William Dillon |
| John Gorman | John Gorman |
| Michael Phelan | Michael Phelan |
| James Clohosey | James Clohosey |
| John Kennedy | John Kennedy |
| Thomas Martin | Thomas Martin |
| James Bowe | William Walsh |
| | John Dunne |
| | Patrick Quigley |

*Source: Kilkenny Journal* 7 January and 10 June 1891.

Hennessy's nomination papers the previous December, James Clohosey and Thomas Martin, became members of the Irish National Federation committee.

December 1890 proved decisive in the career of Charles Stewart Parnell and in the development of the home rule movement and the land movement in Ireland. In the *Kilkenny Journal* of 3 December the editor feared that the hopes of the nation would be 'dashed to the ground in the very moment of victory and that the triumphs gained by ten years' hard fighting should be lost in a few hours.'[32] It was presumptuous of the editor to believe that victory for either goal was so near prior to the North Kilkenny by-election of 1890 but hopes were certainly dashed both during and after the election. The editor of the unionist newspaper, the *Kilkenny Moderator*, had cause to bask in the result when he wrote: 'To us Conservatives and Unionists the result of the contest is indeed of no consequence, and the quarrel has had one great result whereof we may rejoice – namely, the smashing of Home Rule.'[33] A further and enduring consequence of the by-election result was the division of the country into Parnellite and anti-Parnellite factions. Nine years would pass before the rift in Tullaroan caused by the Parnell split was healed by the emergence of a new organization – the United Irish League.

On Sunday 27 May 1900 a meeting was held in Tullaroan to consider the question of establishing a branch of the United Irish League in the parish. William Gaffney chaired the meeting. The attendance included James Bowe and Edmond Walshe. The decision reached at the meeting was to defer forming a branch until a national convention was held in June. Before the meeting broke up the members noted that this was the first meeting to be held in the parish since the elected representatives of Kilkenny Co. Council had refused to condemn the British government in their 'unjust and tyrannical war' in South Africa. They called on the constituents of the county councillors to take up the issue with their representatives. Then, ever growing in confidence, Tullaroan 'went international' by adopting the following resolution with a message for the southern hemisphere:

That we tender to the noble burghers of South Africa our sincere good wishes in their heroic struggle for freedom and trust that their noble efforts will be crowned with success and that England's robber flag will be humbled to the dust, defeated and disgraced.[34]

Following this resolution, the local leaders in Tullaroan showed that no stage would be too big for them. Oral tradition in James Bowe's family states that in 1906 he was nominated to take up the vacant seat for the representation of North Kilkenny at Westminster but turned it down in favour of Michael Meagher who had come to prominence initially when James Bowe and he allegedly posted the first boycotting notice in Tullaroan on 5 December 1880.[35] Michael Meagher served as MP for North Kilkenny until 1918.

# Conclusion

The impact of the establishment of the Land League in Tullaroan in December 1880 could hardly have been predicted. Nothing had occurred in the closing years of the 1870s to indicate that the community there was ready to take up the ideals and the tactics of the Land League with such fervour. Yet, in 1880 and 1881 the posting of threatening notices in Tullaroan resulted in the intimidation of neighbours within the community and in the breakdown of good relations with the police. James Bowe's alleged boycotting activities eventually landed him in prison and caused him subsequently to be abandoned by the leadership of the local branch of the Land League in the person of the Revd Patrick Meany, the branch vice-president. The adoption of Land League tactics appears to have been 'too much, too soon' in Tullaroan in 1881. The result of this was a split in the community at the end of the year with Bowe depending on his neighbours from the adjoining parish to help him save his crops. To the credit of those involved the split did not last beyond six months when, according to a newspaper report, James Bowe, now with the elevated status of 'ex-suspect' after his name, and his former protagonist, the Revd Patrick Meany CC, stood side by side at the rehousing of an evicted tenant. The Tullaroan branch of the Ladies' Land League generated a large amount of publicity in the local newspaper for a few short months in 1882. The jailing of nine men in 1888 caused the ladies to observe proudly that this generation of men was capable of 'sustaining the honour of the parish'. Unlike at national level, there is no evidence of animosity between the Ladies' Land League and the men of the parish.

After the Tullaroan branch of the Irish National League was founded in March 1884 the members of the branch adopted the constitutional route to change as opposed to the route that involved boycotting and intimidation. But for the perseverance of the Tullaroan branch in seeking to win control of the board of guardians of Kilkenny poor law union, it is possible that the Kilkenny union would not have had a nationalist chairman at this time. When the branch eventually achieved success, the issue was no longer high on the national agenda; therefore, the members must be credited for not giving up on the campaign.

Land grabbing had an immense impact on the community with the jailing of nine parishioners in 1888. Oral tradition states that the family of the offending tenant, who took the evicted farm, was ostracized long into the new century. James Bowe received his second jail term for land agitation

then. Having spent two terms in jail for his beliefs, Bowe's experiences do
not sustain J.W.H. Carter's claim that many local Land League leaders were
either motivated by a desire for power or were mercenary opportunists who
appropriated the land movement. The way in which the land movement
brought about positive change in the community was demonstrated when the
parishioners came together in the spring of 1888 to sow the crops for the
families of the prisoners. When James Bowe was imprisoned first in 1881, he
had to depend on his friends in the neighbouring parish to save his crops.

The analysis of the North Kilkenny by-election of 1890 highlights the
growth of confidence, and, therefore one of the major changes, brought about
by the land movement in Tullaroan in the period 1879–91. Of all the occasions
when the Tullaroan branch 'begged to take the initiative', when important
issues arose in the county, perhaps the most remarkable was the attempt to put
a local candidate in place for the by-election before the Irish Party made its
choice known. The attempt was superseded when an election convention was
hastily organized in Kilkenny city but the occasion demonstrated the level of
involvement to which local leaders in Tullaroan now aspired. The politicisation
of Tullaroan in the 1890s was a legacy from involvement in the 'politics' of the
land movement during the previous decade. To this day it is a highly politicized
parish. The Parnell split was emphasized in Tullaroan when the poor law union
elections came round in March 1891. It was the only parish in the Kilkenny
union where an election was required in three electoral divisions in order to
return a guardian. In each of the divisions a Parnellite candidate faced an anti-
Parnellite candidate. In only one was the Parnellite candidate successful and
that was by default, due to an objection being lodged against the anti-
Parnellite, but Parenell's supporters in Tullaroan, though in the minority, were
obviously intent on maintaining their loyalty to the end.

During the closing decades of the twentieth century, and into the new
century, historians changed the focus of study of the land movement from
the prominent leaders to the social background of both sides in the movement, that is, the tenants and their holdings and the landlords and their
estates. It is opportune now to change the emphasis of study again, this time
to the local leaders, their families, friends, neighbours and protagonists in
order to broaden our understanding of one of the great mass movements in
European history. In the major studies of Irish nationalism the importance of
localism can easily be missed unless purposefully pursued.

# Notes

| | | | |
|---|---|---|---|
| CSORP | Chief Secretary's Office Registered Papers | NAI | National Archives of Ireland |
| | | MP | Member of Parliament |
| DED | District Electoral Division | RM | Resident Magistrate |
| FJ | *Freeman's Journal* | PLG | Poor Law Guardian |
| JP | Justice of the Peace | RC | Roman Catholic |
| KJ | *Kilkenny Journal* | RIC | Royal Irish Constabulary |
| KM | *Kilkenny Moderator* | | |

## INTRODUCTION

1 William L. Feingold, 'Land League power: the Tralee poor law election of 1881' in Samuel Clarke and James S. Donnelly (eds), *Irish peasants, violence and political unrest, 1780–1914* (Manchester and Wisconsin, 1983), pp 285–310.

## 1. THE ESTABLISHMENT OF THE LAND LEAGUE IN TULLAROAN

1 *KJ*, 6 Nov. 1880.
2 Gerard Moran, 'William Scully and Ballycohey: a fresh look' in *Tipperary Historical Journal* (1992), pp 63–74.
3 *KJ*, 11 Dec. 1880.
4 *KJ*, 11 Dec. 1880.
5 J.W.H. Carter, *The land war and its leaders in Queen's County, 1879–82* (Portlaoise, 1994), p. 93.
6 *FJ*, 3 Nov., 29 Dec. 1880.
7 *KJ*, 2 Feb. 1881.

## 2. BOYCOTTING, IMPRISONMENT AND DIVISION IN TULLAROAN

1 RIC Constable James McElhoney's report, 28 May 1881 (NAI, CSORP 1881/44511).

2 Threatening letter, 24 Dec. 1880, (NAI, CSORP, 1881/44511).
3 Theodore W. Moody, *Davitt and Irish revolution, 1846–82* (Oxford, 1981), p. 420.
4 Sub-Inspector Lawless' report, 1 Jan. 1881 (NAI, CSORP, 1881/44511).
5 Constable McElhoney's report, 28 May 1881 (NAI, CSORP 1881/44511).
6 Sub-Inspector Lawless' report, 22 April 1881 (NAI, CSORP 1881/17969).
7 Sub-inspector Lawless' report, 24 April 1881 (NAI, CSORP 1881/17969).
8 Sub-Inspector Lawless' report 27 April 1881 (NAI, CSORP 1881/17969).
9 A reference to the 1831 affray in Carrickshock, Co. Kilkenny when resistance to the payment of tithes resulted in civilian and police deaths.
10 Constable McElhoney's police report, 2 May 1881 (NAI, CSORP, 1881/44511).
11 Ibid.
12 *KJ*, 13 July 1881.
13 Constable McElhoney's report, 9 May 1881 (NAI, CSORP, 1881/44511).
14 Ibid.
15 Sub-Inspector Lawless' report, 11 May 1881 (NAI, CSORP 1881/44511).

16 Constable McElhoney's report, 9 May 1881 (NAI, CSORP, 1881/44511).
17 Threatening letter, 17 May 1881 (NAI, CSORP, 1881/44511).
18 Moody, *Davitt*, p. 363.
19 Resident Magistrate William Hort's report [hereafter cited as RM Hort], 19 May 1881 (NAI, CSORP, 1881/44511).
20 RM Hort's report, 19 June 1881, (NAI, CSOPRP, 1881/44511).
21 Constable McElhoney's report, 28 May 1881 (NAI, CSORP, 1881/44511).
22 Constable McElhoney's report, 28 May 1881 (NAI, CSORP, 1881/44511).
23 Virginia Crossman, *Politics, law and order in nineteenth-century Ireland* (Dublin, 1996), p. 222.
24 Sub-Inspector Lawless' report, 13 June 1881 (NAI, CSORP, 1881/44511).
25 Warrant to arrest James Bowe, 9 June 1881 (NAI, CSORP, 1881/44511).
26 Sub-Inspector Lawless' report, 4 May 1881 (NAI, CSORP, 1881/44511).
27 Mrs Walshe to Mrs McElhoney, 19 June 1881 (NAI, CSORP, 1881/44511).

28 Mrs Walshe to Constable Morrissey, 19 June 1881 (NAI, CSORP, 1881/44511).
29 Constable McElhoney's report, 28 May 1881 (NAI, CSORP, 1881/44511).
30 RM Hort's report, 19 June 1881 (NAI, CSORP, 1881/44511).
31 RM Hort's report 8 July 1881 (NAI, CSORP, 1881/44511).
32 Ibid.
33 Petition from Register No. 84, H.M. Prison, Naas, 7 July 1881 (NAI, CSORP, 1881/44511).
34 Sub-Inspector Lawless' report, 18 July 1881 (NAI, CSORP, 1881/44511).
35 Ibid.
36 Sub-Inspector Lawless' report, 19 July 1881 (NAI, CSORP, 1881/44511).
37 Ibid.
38 Cancelled books, Irish Valuation Office: DED, Ballybeagh; parish, Tullaroan; barony, Crannagh; county, Kilkenny.
39 RM Hort's letter, 18 July 1881 (NAI, CSORP, 1881/44511).
40 Ibid.
41 Sub-Inspector Lawless' report, 30 July 1881 (NAI, CSORP, 1881/44511).
42 Sub-Inspector Lawless' report, 11 Aug. 1881 (NAI, CSORP, 1881/44511).
43 Constable McElhoney's report, 22 Aug. 1881 (NAI, CSORP, 1881/44511).
44 Hand writing expert John Shaw Peake's report, 20 August 1881 (NAI, CSORP, 1881/44511).
45 Constable McElhoney's report, 22 Aug. 1881 (NAI, CSORP, 1881/44511).
46 RM Hort's report, 23 Aug. 1881 (NAI, CSORP, 1881/44511).
47 Carter, *Queen's Co.*, p. 147.
48 Constable McElhoney's report, 22 Aug. 1881 (NAI, CSORP, 1881/44511).
49 Sub-Inspector Lawless' report, 3 Oct. 1881 (NAI, CSORP, 1881/44511).
50 RM Hort's report, 7 Oct. 1881 (NAI, CSORP, 1881/44511).
51 County Inspector Gibbons' letter, 13 Oct. 1881 (NAI, CSORP, 1881/44511).
52 Constable Doyle's report, 14 Oct. 1881 (NAI, CSORP, 1881/44511).
53 RM Hort's report, 19 Oct. 1881 (NAI, CSORP, 1881/44511).
54 Government paper, 27 Oct. 1881 (NAI, CSORP, 1881/44511).
55 Governor's letter from Naas Prison, 28 Oct. 1881 (NAI, CSORP, 1881/44511).
56 Head Constable Depo's report, 8 Nov. 1881 (NAI, CSORP, 1881/44511).
57 County Inspector Read's minute on Constable Doyle's report, 9 Nov. 1881 (NAI, CSORP, 1881/44511).
58 Carter, *Queen's Co.*, p. 210.
59 Head Constable Depo's report, 12 Nov. 1881 (NAI, CSORP, 1881/44511).
60 *KJ*, 7 Dec. 1881.
61 Head Constable Depo's report, 25 Nov. 1881 (NAI, CSORP, 1881/44511).
62 Ibid.
63 S.J. Connolly (ed), *The Oxford companion to Irish history* (Oxford, 1998), p. 300.
64 Head Constable Depo's report, 13 Dec. 1881 (NAI, CSORP, 1881/44511).

3. THE LADIES' LAND LEAGUE AND THE 'RUTHLESS HAND OF THE EVICTOR'

1 Moody, *Davitt*, p. 457.
2 Carter, *Queen's Co.*, p. 283.
3 Mrs Walshe to Mrs McElhoney, 19 June 1881 (NAI, CSORP, 1881/44511).
4 Carter, *Queen's Co.*, p. 242.
5 *KJ*, 29 April 1882.
6 *KJ*, 22 July 1882.
7 *KJ*, 22 July 1882.
8 Anna Parnell, *The tale of a great sham*, ed. Dana Hearne (Dublin, 1986), p. 151.
9 *KJ*, 22 July 1882.
10 *KJ*, 2 Aug. 1882.
11 Donal J. O'Sullivan, *The Irish constabularies* (Dingle, 1999), p. 159.
12 *KJ*, 2 Aug. 1882.
13 RM Hort's report, 23 Aug. 1881 (NAI, CSORP, 1881/44511).
14 Carter, *Queen's Co.*, p. 283.
15 *KJ*, 2 Sept. 1882.
16 Parnell, *Great sham*, p. 24.
17 *KJ*, 8 Dec. 1883.

4. THE IMPACT OF THE IRISH NATIONAL LEAGUE ON TULLAROAN

1 *KJ*, 8 March 1884.
2 James S. Donnelly Jnr, *The land and the people of nineteenth-century Cork* (London and Boston, 1975), p. 315.
3 Laurence Geary, 'Parnell and the Irish Land Question' in Donal McCartney (ed.) *Parnell: the politics of power* (Dublin 1991), pp 90–101.
4 *KJ*, 22 March 1884.
5 *KJ*, 29 March 1884.
6 *KJ*, 19 April 1884.
7 *KJ*, 3 May 1884.
8 *KJ*, 7 May 1884.
9 *KJ*, 24 May 1884.
10 Virginia Crossman, *Local government in nineteenth-century Ireland* (Belfast 1994), p. 43.
11 *KJ*, 21 June 1884.
12 *KJ*, 21 June 1884.
13 *KJ*, 3 Dec. 1884.
14 *KJ*, 6 Dec. 1884.
15 *KJ*, 10 Jan. 1885.
16 *KJ*, 4 April 1885.
17 *KJ*, 22 April 1885.
18 *KJ*, 24 March 1886.
19 *KJ*, 27 March 1886.
20 *KJ*, 3 April 1886.

21 *KM*, 31 March 1886.
22 *KJ*, 31 March 1886.
23 *KJ*, 3 April 1886.
24 *KJ*, 30 Oct. 1886.
25 *KJ*, 23 Oct. 1886.
26 *KJ*, 23 Oct. 1886.
27 *KJ*, 30 Oct. 1886.
28 *KJ*, 2 Feb. 1887.
29 *KJ*, 12 Feb. 1887.
30 *KJ*, 16 Feb. 1887.
31 *KJ*, 23 Feb. 1887.
32 Minutes of meeting of board of guardians, Kilkenny poor law union, 31 March 1887 (Kilkenny county library).
33 *KJ*, 2 April 1887.
34 Minutes of board of guardians meeting, Kilkenny poor law union, 31 March 1887 (Kilkenny county library).
35 *KJ*, 2 April 1887.
36 Crossman, *Politics*, p. 226.
37 William L. Feingold, *The revolt of the tenantry: the transformation of local government in Ireland 1872–86* (Boston, 1984), p. 234.

5. THE 'TULLAROAN THIRTEEN'

1 *KJ*, 31 March 1888.
2 Cancelled books, Irish Valuation Office: townland, Adamstown; D.E.D. Rathealy; parish, Tullaroan; barony, Crannagh; county Kilkenny.
3 *KJ*, 31 March 1888.
4 Donnelly, *Nineteenth-century Cork*, p. 328.
5 *KJ*, 28 March 1888.
6 Cancelled books, Irish Valuation Office; parish, Tullaroan; barony, Crannagh; county Kilkenny.
7 *KJ*, 28 March 1888.
8 NAI, CSORP, 1888/21065.
9 RIC County Inspector John Sheehan's report, 28 March

1888 (NAI, CSORP, 1888/6746).
10 *KJ*, 31 March 1888.
11 *Thom's almanac and official directory of the United Kingdom and Ireland* (Dublin 1888), pp 1098–1101.
12 *KJ*, 31 March 1888.
13 *KJ*, 4 April 1888.
14 *KJ*, 4 April 1888.
15 *KJ*, 7 April 1888.
16 *KJ*, 7 April 1888.
17 *KJ*, 11 April 1888.
18 Cancelled books, Irish Valuation Office: county: Kilkenny; barony: Crannagh; parish: Tullaroan; townland, Adamstown; D.E.D., Rathealy.
19 Outrage report, 10 Aug. 1888, (NAI, INL proceedings, box 10).
20 Interview with Mr Michael Kirk, grandson of James Bowe, 10 April 2003.
21 *KJ*, 21 April 1888.
22 *KJ*, 21 April 1888.
23 *KJ*, 2 May 1888.
24 *KJ*, 23 May 1888.
25 *KJ*, 23 May 1888.
26 *KJ*, 9 June 1888.
27 *KJ*, 22 Aug. 1888.
28 *KJ*, 29 Aug. 1888
29 *KJ*, 1 Sept. 1888.
30 *KJ*, 20 March 1889.
31 Laurence Geary, *Plan of campaign 1886–91* (Cork, 1985), p. 123.
32 *KJ*, 16 Nov. 1889.
33 *FJ*, 7 Oct. 1889.
34 *KJ*, 19 Nov. 1890.

6. THE IMPACT OF THE PARNELL SPLIT ON TULLAROAN

1 Alan O'Day, *Charles Stewart Parnell* (Dundalk, 1988), p. 69.

2 Paul Bew, *Charles Stewart Parnell* (2nd. ed., Dublin, 1991), p. 110.
3 *KJ*, 1 Jan. 1890.
4 *KJ*, 16 July 1890.
5 *KJ*, 19 Nov. 1890.
6 *KJ*, 19 Nov. 1890.
7 *KJ*, 19 Nov. 1890.
8 *KJ*, 21 Nov. 1890.
9 *KJ*, 29 Nov. 1890.
10 *KJ*, 29 Nov. 1890.
11 Bew, *Parnell*, p. 117.
12 *KJ*, 3 Dec. 1890.
13 *KJ*, 6 Dec. 1890.
14 *KJ*, 10 Dec. 1890.
15 *KJ*, 10 Dec. 1890.
16 Marie Louise Legg, *Newspapers and nationalism: the Irish provincial press, 1850–92* (Dublin 1999), p. 145.
17 *KJ*, 20 Dec. 1890.
18 *KJ*, 13 Dec. 1890.
19 *KJ*, 10 Dec. 1890.
20 Moran, 'Scully' in Tipperary Historical Journal (1992), pp 63–74.
21 *KJ*, 13 Dec. 1890.
22 *KM*, 17 Dec. 1890.
23 Interview with Mr Dick Walshe, grandson of Edmond Walshe, 12 Nov. 2002.
24 *KJ*, 17 Dec. 1890.
25 *KJ*, 24 Dec. 1890.
26 Interview with Mr Michael Kirk, grandson of James Bowe, 12 December 2002.
27 *KJ*, 7 Feb. 1891.
28 *KJ*, 11 Feb. 1891.
29 *KJ*, 11 Feb. 1891.
30 *KJ*, 10 Oct. 1891.
31 *KJ*, 10 June 1891.
32 *KJ*, 3 Dec. 1890.
33 *KM*, 24 Dec. 1890.
34 *KJ*, 2 June 1900.
35 Interview with Mr Michael Kirk, grandson of James Bowe, 12 Dec. 2002.